LIGHTHOUSES OF THE SOUTH WEST

A definitive guide

ROBIN JONES

HALSGROVE

First published in Great Britain in 2011.

*Pictures marked thus are published under a Creative Commons licence,
the full details of which can be found at www.creativecommons.org

To Jenny, Ross and Vicky

British Library Cataloguing-in-Publication Data
A CIP record for this title is available from the British Library

ISBN 978 0 85704 107 4

HALSGROVE
Halsgrove House,
Ryelands Industrial Estate,
Bagley Road, Wellington, Somerset TA21 9PZ
Tel: 01823 653777   Fax: 01823 216796
email: sales@halsgrove.com

Part of the Halsgrove group of companies
Information on all Halsgrove titles is available at: www.halsgrove.com

Printed in China by Everbest Printing Co Ltd

CONTENTS

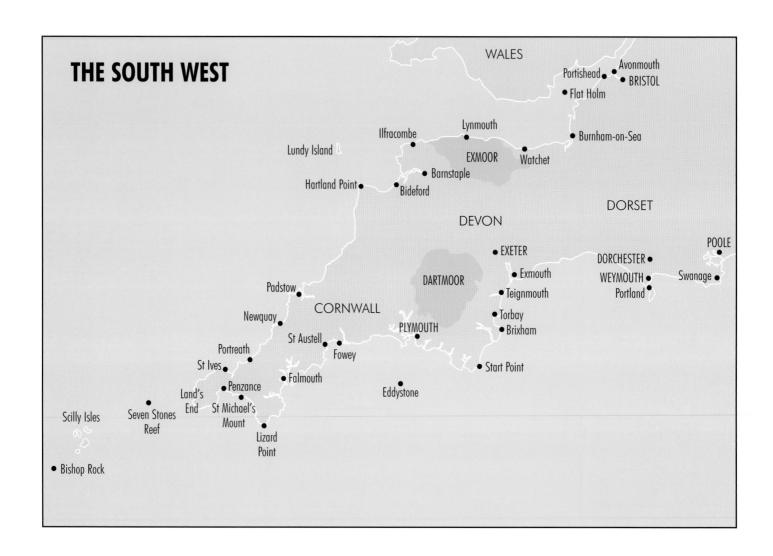

THE SOUTH WEST

WALES

Avonmouth
Portishead •• BRISTOL
• Flat Holm

Lynmouth
Ilfracombe •
• Burnham-on-Sea
Lundy Island
EXMOOR • Watchet

Hartland Point • • Barnstaple
• Bideford

DORSET

DEVON

• EXETER
DARTMOOR
• Exmouth
DORCHESTER •
POOLE

Padstow
• Teignmouth
WEYMOUTH •
• Swanage
CORNWALL
• Torbay
Portland
Newquay •
PLYMOUTH •
• Brixham

St Austell •
Portreath
• Fowey
• Start Point
St Ives •
• Penzance
Falmouth
Land's
End
• Eddystone
Seven Stones
St Michael's
Scilly Isles
Reef
Mount

Lizard
Point

• Bishop Rock

The first and last place in Britain: Bishop Rock lighthouse. TIM DOBSON*

Anvil Point on the Planet Lighthouse! DAVE JOHNSON

INTRODUCTION

FEW OF THE WORLD'S coastlines can boast not only as many lighthouses as that of south-west England, but their sheer variety in shape, size, design and ancestry.

For millennia, the sheer cliffs with jagged rocks at their feet facing the full force of the Atlantic surge showed no mercy as generations of sailors attempted to navigate the major trade route.

Fiercest of all was the rounding of Land's End, the extreme south-westernmost point of the British mainland, overlooking the great expanse where three seas met – the Atlantic, the English Channel and Irish Sea, and the producing of the great swell which would never hesitate in tossing ships like a cork on the ocean, so often sending them to their doom on the isolated pinnacles of Wolf Rock, the Longships or the Seven Stones reef.

We do not know whether the Phoenicians who came to Cornwall to barter for tin or the Romans who sought the mineral wealth of the Mendip Hills had navigational aids around the coast. Indeed, nobody knows who built the world's first lighthouse, but the oldest one recorded was the great Pharos of Alexandria, built around 200 BC.

Britain's oldest lighthouse is to be found at Dover Castle, and dates from AD 90.

Two millennia ago, the population of the south-west peninsula, and indeed that of Europe as a whole, was but a fraction of that of modern times. Even if they had been familiar with lighthouse technology, who in medieval times would go to the expense of building one on these shores, especially as they were just as likely to guide a hostile incursion from France or Spain into a port ripe for ransacking as to help friendly ships?

Nonetheless, it is this selfsame ruthless coast which prompted great developments in lighthouse technology, which brought multiple benefits to shipping lanes everywhere around the globe. The innovations of engineering genius John Smeaton manifested in the third Eddystone lighthouse, the world's first stone lighthouse tower at sea, and the towering achievement that is James Walker and Sir James Douglass's Bishop's Rock lighthouse, guarding the western approach to Britain, crown the multitude of feats of technological inspiration and matchless endurance that produced stone towers and saved countless lives around the beautiful but treacherous coasts of the West Country.

The story of the development of lighthouses around the south west begins with the crude beacons and braziers that were lit on hills to guide fishermen home, and ended with the

The Harwich headquarters of Trinity House, from where all of its automated lighthouses including those in this book are controlled today. TRINITY HOUSE

A *structure which revolutionised lighthouse building was John Smeaton's third Eddystone lighthouse, the top of which now stands on Plymouth Hoe.* JAMES CRIDLAND

The control room in the Trinity House headquarters in Harwich now fulfils the role long undertaken by lighthouse keepers. TRINITY HOUSE

automation of all the Trinity House lighthouses and their control by telemetry link from the Trinity House Operations Control Centre at Harwich in Essex, as modern technology completely replaced the time-honoured manual operation.

From afar it might seem romantic, but few would seriously envy the job of a keeper at a rock station (as lighthouses at sea are called), living for weeks or even months at a time in the very cramped conditions of a circular tower, washing in a bucket, sleeping in a curved bunk bed, throwing the contents of the toilet bucket from the top gallery ensuring that the wind is in the 'right' direction, and if your fellow keepers' habits got on your nerves...

The modern era of lighthouses began firstly with the building of the Eddystone lighthouse by the ill-fated Henry Winstanley in 1695 and secondly with Scotland's Bell Rock lighthouse in Scotland by Robert Stevenson in 1810.

Trinity House, the organisation which operates Britain's lighthouses, is believed to have its origins in a twelfth-century charitable guild founded by Archbishop of Canterbury Stephen Langton, who played a key role in King John signing the Magna Carta.

However, the first official record of the name is the granting of a Royal Charter by Henry VIII in 1514 to a group of seafarers under the name "The Master, Wardens, and Assistants of

the Guild, Fraternity, or Brotherhood of the most glorious and undivided Trinity, and of St Clement in the Parish of Deptford-Strond in the County of Kent" "so that they might regulate the pilotage of ships in the King's streams".

The name of the guild came from the church of Holy Trinity and St Clement, which adjoined the king's new dockyard at Deptford. The first master of the guild was Thomas Spert, captain of Henry's flagship *Mary Rose*.

Under the Seamarks Act 1566, Trinity House was empowered to establish "So many beacons, marks and signs for the sea whereby the dangers may be avoided and escaped and ships the better come into their ports without peril."

The first lighthouse built by Trinity House was at Lowestoft in 1609, one of a chain of lights to guide vessels through Norfolk sandbanks. After this, many lighthouses sprang up around the shores of Britain, many built by private entrepreneurs who leased the right to operate them from Trinity House, and extracted fees from passing ships. The quality of many of these lights left much to be desired; legislation was passed in 1836 for them to be compulsory purchased and handed over to Trinity House.

Numerous early navigational aids were often no more than lamps lit in high windows by holy men. Braziers on top of towers came later, but often they emitted so much smoke that they often became invisible from the sea.

In the first three Eddystone lighthouses, candles provided an alternative: Smeaton's tower had 24 candles burning in its lantern. Light intensity is measured in candela, one candela roughly equivalent to one candle: modern lighthouses have an intensity of several hundred thousand candela.

The turning point came in 1782 when Swiss inventor Ami Argand produced the circular wick, which had a current of air passing through the middle, and aided by a glass covering, produced a brighter flame with little smoke. Further developments saw lamps produced with several wicks, each producing a more powerful light.

At first, fish oil was burned in the lamps, but in 1901, Arthur Kitson introduced the pressurised vapour burner, which trebled the brightness.

The magnification of the light takes place through giant arrangements of curved prisms and lenses which weigh several tons - yet which, floating in baths of liquid mercury, can be turned by a small finger.

Early lighthouse lenses, designed to concentrate the light from the lamp, were big, bulky and cumbersome affairs. The biggest advance in lighthouse lens technology is attributed to Frenchman Augustin-Jean Fresnel, who in 1822 produced thinner, larger, and flatter lenses with a larger aperture and shorter focal length, by building them in separate sections rather than as a complete whole.

The Fresnel principle enabled lighthouses to be visible over much greater distances focusing 85 per cent of a lamp's light as opposed to the far less efficient 20 per cent focused

Lighthouses have their own following and as with railways, boats and aircraft, there are ranges of models available to collectors. The Little Dart Company, based in Tiverton, has a range of fine-scale miniatures for collectors: pictured is Smeaton's Tower. LITTLE DART

Visitors are fascinated by the Fresnel optics in the National Maritime Museum Cornwall at Falmouth.
NMMC

The Portland Bill lighthouse looms over the southern tip of Dorset.
ROBIN JONES

using the parabolic reflectors that preceded them.

The first Fresnel lens appeared in 1823 in the Cordouan lighthouse guarding the Gironde estuary, the light of which could be seen over 20 miles away. Not only did Fresnel lenses greatly enhance the effectiveness of lights, but they could fit into more compact spaces.

Fresnel's lighthouse lenses are classified into six orders according to their focal length. The 'order' refers to the optical power of the lens. A first order lens has the largest focal length and is the most powerful and expensive; while a sixth order lens is the smallest. As a rule, the major coastal lighthouses installed first, second or third order lenses, while the smaller harbour lighthouses and beacons have fourth, fifth or sixth order lenses.

Michael Faraday, one of the key figures in the introduction of electricity to technology, was scientific adviser to Trinity House between 1836 and 1865. He introduced the system of fixed continuous higher and lower lights, whereby mariners could check where they were from the relative positions of two fixed points, with rotating lights using Fresnel lenses. Under the new system, each lighthouse emits a beam of light of a set and known duration so that seafarers can fix their location.

In the 1850s, glassmakers Chance Brothers of Smethwick, West Midlands, began making glass of sufficient quality to produce such lenses in Britain rather than importing them from France.

Faraday also oversaw the installation of a system of electric light devised by inventor Frederick Hale Holmes in the South Foreland lighthouse in Kent in 1858. The idea of using electric light bulbs in lighthouse lanterns did not take off for several decades because of the expense involved, but during the twentieth century, electrification slowly became standard practice.

On 26 November 1998, North Foreland in Kent became the last Trinity House lighthouse to be fully automated when the last six keepers stood down at a ceremony attended by the Duke of Edinburgh.

A great era had ended, and twenty-first century developments in satellite navigation systems have led Trinity House to consider making several lighthouses redundant altogether.

However, lighthouses have become an integral part of the British seaside landscape, and are much admired by locals and visitors alike. They have inspired paintings, books, poems, songs and even the name of a chart-topping pop group. In some cases, like Burnham-on-Sea, they have not only contributed to the safety of a port or harbour, but played a key role in its development.

This book is a definitive tour of the lighthouses ancient and modern along the coast from Avonmouth around Land's End to Swanage, and for completeness, includes lightships and also the major daymarks – lightless beacons to guide ships during daytime. As a lifelong lover of the West Country, I have found it a fascinating voyage of discovery, and I hope you will too.

CHAPTER ONE
AVONMOUTH

THE TERM 'THE WEST COUNTRY' conjures up a magical myriad of visions of delights. The pounding Atlantic breakers and the glorious surfing beaches of North Cornwall and North Devon, picture-postcard fishing villages of the English Channel coast, wild rugged untamed Dartmoor and Bodmin Moor and their ponies, the pastel-hued thatched cottages of Devon, countless tales of smugglers, pirates and pixies, historic harbours from where Drake and Raleigh set sail for the new world, cream tea shops and the romance of Daphne du Maurier and Ross Poldark.

It is therefore ironic that Avonmouth, the start of our journey on the eastern bank of the Severn estuary, is unashamedly associated with none of these, and almost certainly never will be.

Avonmouth is totally a no-frills functional and workaday place, given over completely to modern industry, and most visitors to the far west never go there, nor would want to: they merely glimpse at it as they pass by on the M5, the bridge over the Avon offering a grandstand view of the grain warehouses and smoking chimneys of the chemical plants as the river below empties itself into the Severn estuary at a point known as the Swash Channel. Indeed, parts of the locality appear to the untrained eye as a giant chemistry set, and no, it does not have a beach.

The North Pier lighthouse with the second Severn motorway crossing in the distance. BRISTOL PORT COMPANY

The reason for the existence of Avonmouth, a relatively new place, relates to the surfing waves mentioned above. The Atlantic surge is funnelled up the Bristol Channel and the Severn Estuary, creating the third-biggest tidal range in the world after the Bay of Fundy in Newfoundland and the Bay of Ungava in Quebec Province. The net effect is the huge expanses of sand and mudflats that appear at low tide along the upper shore of the Bristol Channel, at places like Weston-super-Mare and Burnham-on-Sea, and which reduce the Avon leading upstream to Bristol, historically one of the world's greatest ports, to a tiny channel weaving its way amongst glistening mud. The greatest difference between low and high water is that at spring tides at Avonmouth which can exceed 47ft – compare and contrast with six feet at Lowestoft to place it in perspective.

So while the Avon is easily navigable by ships at high tide, it becomes impassable at low water. For centuries ships in Bristol's docks would have no option but to run aground, leading to the phrase "shipshape and Bristol fashion" to describe vessels that could withstand being repeatedly stranded on the mud without their hulls being holed.

In the eighteenth century, rapidly-expanding Liverpool threatened Bristol's huge tobacco trade. As a counter measure, engineer William Jessop designed a dam and lock at Hotwells, effectively creating Bristol's Floating Harbour, so ships could stay afloat at all states of the tide.

Yet ships and their cargo continued to increase in size, and the advent of the railways led to the building of a new harbour on the Severn to the west.

Avonmouth Old Dock was opened in 1877 and acquired by Bristol Corporation in 1884. In 1908, the much larger Royal Edward Dock was opened.

The docks were operated by the Port of Bristol Authority, part of Bristol City Council, until 1991. The council then granted a 150-year lease to the Bristol Port Company, which now operates the docks together with Royal Portbury Dock, a deepwater terminal built between 1972-77 near Portishead on the opposite bank of the Avon.

The first lighthouse at Avonmouth preceded the docks. Erected by Trinity House in 1839, its octagonal castellated tower built of stone stood 85ft high. Known as Avon Lighthouse, its traditional fixed white light was lit by oil. The first light was shone on 25 May 1840, and was visible for 14 miles.

The twin lighthouses of Avonmouth Docks: the nearest is the South Pier lighthouse.
BRISTOL PORT COMPANY

Far left: *The modern light inside the South Pier lighthouse's Fresnel lens.*
BRISTOL PORT COMPANY

Left: *The exterior of the South Pier lighthouse's Fresnel lens.*
BRISTOL PORT COMPANY

It was pulled down in 1902 to make way for the Royal Edward Dock. Until that opened, Avonmouth was served by a temporary wooden lighthouse.

The present lighthouses were constructed in 1908 from Norwegian granite, on completion of the Royal Edward Dock.

Both lights are still operational, although not using their original equipment. The North Pier lighthouse, which is 53ft tall, and originally had a wooden lighthouse keeper's hut alongside, is lit by a white LED on a tripod in the gallery, but there is no longer an operational light contained within the Fresnel lens workings.

It has a focal plane of 50ft: a 'focal plane', by the way, is the standard means of 'measuring' lighthouses. It indicates the distance from the water's surface to the middle of the optic.

The South Pier lighthouse, which stands at nearly 30ft high, and has a focal plane of 30ft, is a sectored red and green light using a modern Pharos LED light. A fog signal bell is still operational.

The Avonmouth lighthouses each have a range of 10 nautical miles. Neither piers nor the lighthouses are publicly accessible.

Since the Bristol Port Company took over in 1991, the company's investment of more than £400 million has made it one of the most technically-advanced operators in Europe, handling much larger ships than its competitors elsewhere in southern England.

The South Pier lighthouse.
BRISTOL PORT COMPANY

13

CHAPTER TWO
PORTISHEAD

Blacknore lighthouse is now redundant.
ROBIN JONES

VIEWED FROM A DISTANCE, Portishead is a town that cries out in vain to be a seaside resort. Its foreshore at low tide boasts what seems at first glance to be wide sweeping beaches atypical of the West Country. However, a closer examination reveals the 'sand' to be thick grey Severnside mud and quicksand, and only a slim gritty foreshore behind these mudflats can carry the weight of walkers.

Futile attempts were made to develop Portishead as a resort in the nineteenth century. In 1814, the outer sea wall was built allowing the local marshes to be drained, and in 1830 the Royal Hotel by the pier was built as accommodation catering for travellers on the steamers from Bristol, Wales and Ireland.

Its name meaning 'port at the head of the river', Portishead is colloquially referred to as 'Posset'. Recorded in Roman times, Portishead developed around a small tributary of the Severn estuary near the mouth of the Avon: fishing boats were once tied up where High Street is now.

The town was strategically placed to guard King Road, the name of the estuary waters around Portishead Point, better known as Battery Point. On 31 October 1758, in an encounter off Portishead, HMS *Antelope* captured a French naval ship returning from Quebec.

This headland was so named because a fort was built there by Royalists during the English Civil War but surrendered to the Parliamentarian General Thomas Fairfax in 1645. Guns returned to Battery Point during World War Two.

A pier and a deep-water dock were built by the Bristol & Portishead Pier & Railway to avoid large ships having to sail up the tidal Avon into Bristol. The first ship to tie up at Portishead Dock was the passenger steamer *Lyn*, on 28 June 1879. Bristol Corporation took over the dock in the 1880s.

Landmarks no longer with us are the giant coal-fed power stations built next to the dock, the first in 1926, which later had two 350ft chimney stacks, and the second in 1949. They closed in 1976 and 1982 respectively, and the dock followed in 1992.

It was effectively replaced by the nearby modern Royal Portbury Dock, now a major port for importing motor vehicles.

The old dock was redeveloped into the Port Marine marina. Portishead's stark turnabout from heavy industry to a popular dormitory town for Bristol saw a sizeable upsurge in

Portishead Point or Battery Point lighthouse. ROBIN JONES

The Battery Point memorial to mariners with the lighthouse in the background. ROBIN JONES

population in the early twenty-first century.

Changing times have also affected the town's two lighthouses. The oldest and southernmost, Blacknore or Black Nore, was decommissioned by Trinity House on 27 September 2010.

A superb example of a late Victorian prefabricated lighthouse, it was erected in 1894 to assist shipping in and out of Avonmouth, and was converted to electricity and automated in 1941. Further modifications were made in 2000.

Standing 36ft tall, and with a focal plane of 36ft, its circular six-legged cast iron tower has an enclosed watch room, gallery and lantern with Fresnel lens which gave two flashes of white every ten seconds. It can be reached via the coastal footpath.

A later 30ft-high prefabricated lighthouse with a focal range of 30ft was built at Battery Point in March 1931 by Chance Brothers of Smethwick, and is maintained by the Bristol Port Company. The only surviving example of its type, it comprises a black-painted square pyramidal skeletal tower with a partially-enclosed gallery.

The lighthouse gives three quick white flashes every ten seconds and has a range of 16 nautical miles. An elevated walkway links it to the headland, a public open space reached via Esplanade Road.

On 25 July 1998, the massive two-ton bronze fog bell suspended from the Portishead Point lighthouse was airlifted off amidst concerns that the structure could no longer hold its weight. The bell was replaced by an automated fog horn.

Years later, Portishead shop worker Carol Thomas campaigned to return the bell to the town. The port company accordingly gave it to the town council.

Affixed to a stone monument on the headland above the lighthouse is a plaque highlighting the fact that it is thought to be the nearest point to publicly accessible land in Britain that large ships pass. The monument is dedicated to sailors who over the centuries passed Battery Point on their outward voyages never to return. It was from near here in 1497 that explorer John Cabot set sail on the *Matthew* to Newfoundland.

Edwardian ladies beachcombing on the little stony cove where Blacknore lighthouse stands. ROBIN JONES COLLECTION

30071   Portishead. The Lighthouse.

CHAPTER THREE
ENGLISH AND WELSH GROUNDS

IN BRISTOL CITY CENTRE'S Bathurst Basin, a long-redundant lightship now serves as the clubhouse of the Cabot Cruising Club.

In its days as a Trinity House light vessel, however, it marked the English and Welsh Grounds, vast sandbanks which appear in the Bristol Channel at low tide about five miles off the coast of Clevedon.

A light vessel, or lightship, is a ship which performs the duties of a lighthouse in waters that are too deep for a permanent structure to be built. At first, lightships used oil lamps which could be run up the mast and lowered for servicing, and later fixed lamps, which were serviced in position, and eventually lighthouse-style Fresnel lenses.

Many Trinity House lightships, including the one manning the position of the English and Welsh Grounds, were eventually replaced by large automated buoys.

The Bristol ship is the *John Sebastian*, LV55 in the Trinity House fleet. Of wooden construction with iron beams, she was built in 1885 and served at several different locations, including Cross Sand at Caister and Owers off Selsey Bill before being moved to English and Welsh Grounds on 14 July 1939. In March 1942 she was taken to Milford Haven for overhaul and laid up in Holyhead Harbour as a spare, before returning to English and Welsh Grounds shortly afterwards.

She served there until 1 September 1953, when she was withdrawn and sold to breakers, who beached her at New Passage in the Severn estuary prior to burning.

When the local hotel landlady, owner of the foreshore rights, threatened legal action, LV55 was taken to Portishead Dock and offered for sale again. Salvation came in the form of the cruising club, which bought her in late 1955, naming her *John Sebastian*. The following year she was towed to her present home in Commercial Road and on 3 May 1959, opened as a clubhouse. The last of the timber-built lightships of her type to survive, her deck fittings and interior equipment have long since gone.

In the Bristol Channel, LV55 was replaced by LV72, a steel lightship built by John Crown & Sons of Sunderland in 1903 and possibly the only one powered by both oil and electricity during her working life.

Carrying the name *Juno*, LV72 was one of two lightships in action on D-Day on 6 June 1944, marking a safe passage through a minefield for the Allies' landing craft on their way to

LV72, which served on English & Welsh Grounds, in action on D-Day.
TRINITY HOUSE

the Normandy invasion beaches.

Her posting at the English and Welsh Grounds was her longest, although during 1954 she broke adrift from her moorings and tugs had to reposition her before she ran aground.

Decommissioned in Swansea 1972, she was sold for scrap to the Steel Supply Company. LV72 was not cut up but was painted yellow and used as the company's office before being abandoned in a berth alongside the scrapyard in Neath Abbey Wharf near Swansea where she remains to this day, despite earlier plans to convert her into a nightclub.

However, she is listed by the National Historic Ships Unit as part of the National Register of Historic Ships, making her officially recognised to be of maritime importance and therefore worthy of preservation.

Former Bristol Channel lightship LV55 John Sebastian *in Bathurst Basin.* MATT BUCK*

CHAPTER FOUR
FLAT HOLM

FLAT HOLM HAS BEEN the southernmost part of Wales ever since it became part of the country when Henry I's son Robert Fitzhamon established Glamorganshire in the wake of the Norman Conquest. However, like its English sister Steep Holm, it is a western outlier of Somerset's limestone Mendip Hills, and as its lighthouse guards the busy Bristol shipping lanes, it is therefore included in this volume.

The first light on Flat Holm was a basic brazier mounted on a wooden frame on the higher eastern part of the island plateau, but the Society of Merchant Venturers of Bristol repeatedly complained about its inadequacy.

In 1733, the society's John Elbridge petitioned Trinity House for a better light on the island because of the dangers in the channel. Two years later, William Crispe of Bristol informed Trinity House that he had leased the island, which lies central to the shipping lanes, for 99 years from the Earl of Bute, and offered to build a lighthouse at his own expense. He was also turned down.

Matters reached a head in 1736 when 60 soldiers drowned when their ship was wrecked on the nearby Wolves rocks. Crispe presented a new scheme to the Merchant Venturers on 17 March 1737 and received backing for another bid to Trinity House.

The Merchant Venturers insisted that Crispe stumped up £900 of the necessary finance in return for a lease at £5 a year. He agreed, and the first light was shone on 1 December 1737. The circular stone tower was hit badly in a severe gale which ravaged the West Country on 22 December 1790. The keeper's report said: "We expected every moment to be our last. At three o'clock on the morning of the 23rd, the tower was struck by lightning. The man attending the fire was knocked down and narrowly escaped falling through the stairway. The iron fire grate was smashed to pieces and the top of the tower considerably damaged." The broken light was temporarily replaced by a fire in front of the tower.

On 17 November 1819, Trinity House agreed with principal lessee William Dickenson to take over the light in return for an annual payment of £400. Subsequently, in 1819, the tower was raised from 69ft to 89ft while also being upgraded to house a more powerful fountain oil lantern.

The new fixed white light was shone on 7 September 1820. Two years later, an Act of Parliament gave Trinity House the power to buy outright the leases of any coastal lighthouse and Flat Holm's, the last British signal station in private ownership, was purchased from

Flat Holm lighthouse today, showing the solar panels that power it. FLAT HOLM PROJECT

Flat Holm has a diameter of about 2,000ft with the plateau that gives it its name standing about 70ft above sea level. FLAT HOLM PROJECT

The ruins of the cholera sanatorium, with the lighthouse in the distance. FLAT HOLM PROJECT

The restored foghorn station. FLAT HOLM PROJECT

Dickenson in 1823.

More improvements in 1825 included the raising of the lantern by another 5ft.

In 1867 a 13ft diameter lantern was installed while a clockwork mechanism to rotate the light was installed in 1881, converting it to occulting. This lantern remained in use until 1969. A Douglass incandescent burner installed in 1904 was replaced by a Hood petroleum vapour burner in 1923.

In 1908 a powerful compressed air fog signal having two horns was installed in a separate new building. Originally powered by an engine, the siren gave two blasts in quick succession at two-minute intervals and was heard distinctly by people on both English and Welsh coasts. The foghorn building now has Grade 2 listed status.

Renovations carried out in 1929 when the lighthouse was converted to a rock station included the provision of accommodation for four keepers.

In 1988, the 98ft tall lighthouse, which has a focal plane of 164ft, became fully automated and the keepers were sent back to the mainland for good.

In 1997, the light was modernised and converted to solar power and like all other Trinity House lighthouses in England and Wales, is now controlled from Harwich.

Volunteers from the Flat Holm Society restored the foghorn and engines, and the foghorn station was officially reopened by the Welsh Secretary and the Welsh Assembly First

Secretary in May 2000 when the horn was sounded for the first time in 12 years.

The 100-watt lantern has a white and red group flashing every 10 seconds: the range of the white light is 15 nautical miles, and the red 12 nautical miles.

Day trips to Flat Holm, a designated Local Nature Reserve managed by Cardiff Council, can be made from Barry Island aboard the Flat Holm Project's boat *Lewis Alexander*.

Because of their strategic position on the Bristol Channel, and unfounded fears growing about the installation of Napoleon III as head of state in France, a series of gun emplacements were built on Flat and Steep Holm in the 1860s as part of a line of defences of southern England, known as Palmerston Forts; several of the massive Victorian cannon can still be seen.

A pavilion-style building for cholera patients was built in 1896 as an isolation hospital for Cardiff, so sick sailors could be taken off boats before they reached the port. It stands in ruins today.

A seagull-dominated designated Site of Special Scientific Interest, Flat Holm achieved international fame on 13 May 1897 when 22-year-old Italian inventor Guglielmo Marconi, assisted by Cardiff post office engineer George Kemp, transmitted the world's first wireless signals over open sea from the island to Lavernock Point on the Welsh coast, from a 160ft tall mast. The Morse code message "Are you ready?" began the modern global communications industry, which a century later superseded much lighthouse technology. A monument to Marconi stands on the island's centre.

Guglielmo Marconi.
FLAT HOLM PROJECT

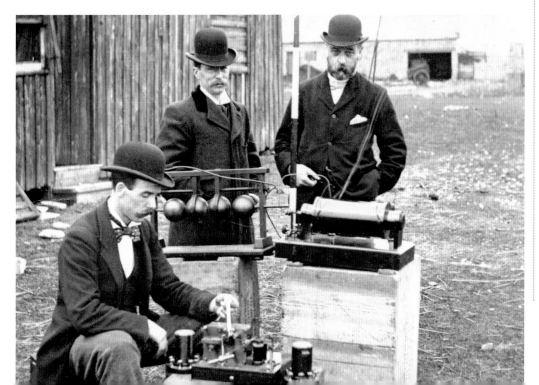

Post office engineers check Marconi's Equipment in 1897. FLAT HOLM PROJECT

CHAPTER FIVE
BURNHAM-ON-SEA

Burnham's first lighthouse, the fourteenth-century parish church of St Andrew, is also Somerset's version of the Leaning Tower of Pisa, as it tilts at 3ft to the horizontal, a factor attributed to poor foundations.
ROBIN JONES

NOT ONLY HAS BURNHAM-ON-SEA had four lighthouses in its history, but it came into existence largely because of them.

The distinctive feature of Burnham is its sweeping sands, which run for seven miles north to Brean Down. Beyond the sands, however, at low tide appears an even bigger expanse of soft sand, mudflats and quicksand, forever a great danger to shipping. Over the Gore Sand, a particularly treacherous sandbank where the River Parrett meets the Bristol Channel, the sea can recede for one-and-a-half miles because of the huge tidal range.

Nobody knows exactly when efforts to prevent loss of life on the shifting sandbanks by shining a light began.

One story relates that in the 1750s, a Burnham sailor's wife lit a candle in the window of their house to guide his ship home through raging seas one stormy night. Other sailors subsequently agreed to pay the woman a fee to keep her light shining.

Another version relates that local curate the Reverend David Davies saw a business opportunity, and bought the rights to the light from the woman.

Yet another tale has it that a navigational light was placed on the top of the fourteenth-century tower of St Andrews church during the eighteenth century. A local vicar, either John Goulden in 1764 or Walter Harris in 1799, then asked the local population to contribute towards the building of a proper lighthouse to replace and improve upon the light from the church tower, the story runs. Accordingly, Davies gave the verger £20 to agree to build the four-storey Round Tower as an extension to his nearby house.

Davies reached agreement with Trinity House in 1813 for a 100-year lease to continue his lighthouse business for £135 a year. Around 1829, Trinity House repurchased the remainder of the lease. The minister then used the money from the sale to build a spa in a bid to boost Burnham's popularity as a visitor destination.

He sank wells near the seafront and discovered two mineral springs, one saline chalybeate, the other sulphur, and built a bath-house above them: the Regency building, named Stert House, is today a listed structure.

Davies hoped that Burnham might become another Cheltenham, Tunbridge Wells or Leamington. However, the spa resort scheme did not take off because the odour from the waters was foul, described as like "that of a cesspool, mixed with an odour not unlike bad horseradish."

Nonetheless, Davies generated sufficient publicity to add Burnham to the embryonic tourist map, and so laid the foundations of today's family seaside resort.

While Trinity House made improvements to the Round Tower, far better navigational aids were clearly needed.

In 1832, a pair of lighthouses was built for Trinity House in succession by contractor Joseph Nelson to help guide ships into the Parrett estuary. The first was Burnham High Light, a slender but domineering structure alongside Berrow Road behind the sand dunes, described by Trinity House as an "elegant lofty structure", and at first powered by a paraffin lamp.

Eight men used wooden scaffold poles, ropes and pulleys, to lift the massive blue stone blocks up its eight storeys. A workman fell to his death while building the tower. It is believed that the great engineer Isambard Kingdom Brunel, whose Bristol & Exeter Railway ran through nearby Highbridge, viewed the construction.

Once built, it was found that it had too low a vantage point, taking into account the huge tidal range. So another was built to supplement it, on the seaward side of the dunes 500 yards

The distinctive 'lighthouse on stilts' which stands in the middle of Burnham's sandy beach.
ROBIN JONES

The High or Pillar lighthouse in Berrow Road which stands sentinel behind the dunes, and a close up of the gallery. ROBIN JONES

to the east. Burnham Low Light, which stands in the middle of the beach itself, is surrounded by water at high tide.

The pair were designed to line up with each other and work in tandem, but are certainly unalike twins. The 99ft tall High or Pillar lighthouse, which has a focal plane of 23ft, comprises a stone tower with a conical roof and a half gallery on the front, incorporating the keeper's quarters, while the Low Lighthouse is a curious-looking 30ft tall square box-like wooden tower with a conical roof, mounted on nine timber pilings. Its tower has two windows, with the white light mounted in front of the upper window and the directional light inside the lower one.

A local man named Burnett wrote an ode to the 'lighthouse on stilts' on one of its legs:

Nine legs to keep me from running away,
White breeches to keep my legs cool while I stay,
A white scaly jacket to keep my shirt clean,
Two eyes not to see with, but for to be seen,
A hat made of glass to keep my head warm,
A cock perched a'top to wake me at morn,
Last of all I have got an upright crooked nose,
Through which I'm to sneeze when I'm smoking, I s'pose!

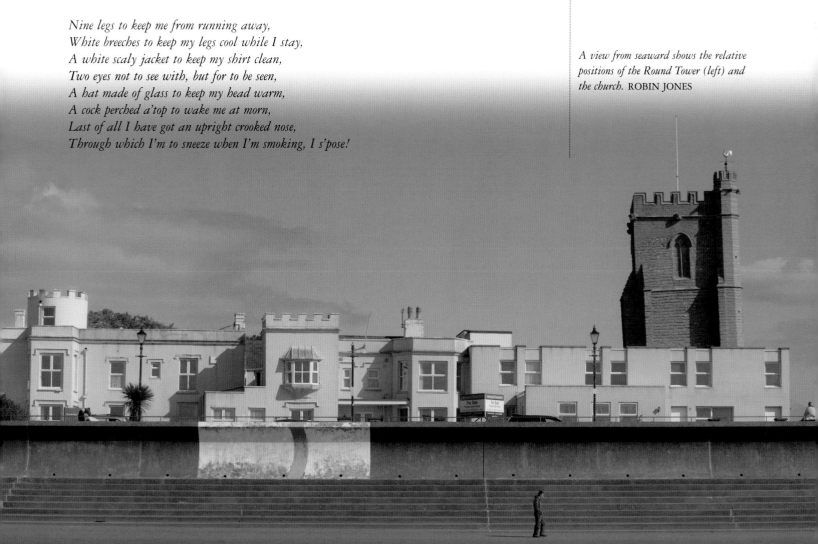

A view from seaward shows the relative positions of the Round Tower (left) and the church. ROBIN JONES

Burnham-on-Sea is renowned for its spectacular sunsets.

The best-known example of a ship which came to grief on the Gore Sand is the Berrow wreck. The Nornen was a wooden Norwegian barque which floundered on the flats while carrying a cargo of resin and turpentine from Georgia to South Wales on 7 January 1897. All 11 crew members and the ship's dog managed to wade ashore, and the ship, stuck where the sand meets quicksand, was broken up, save for the waterlogged hull timbers which are still there on Berrow beach today.
ROBIN JONES

The remains of the Round Tower today.
ROBIN JONES

After the lighthouses were completed, Trinity House ordered that the Round Tower, now redundant as a navigational aid, be reduced by two storeys so it would not be confused with the High Light. After this was done, its new top floor was crenelated to remove any last hint of confusion, and it survives in this form to this day.

The High Light quickly became a trademark of Burnham, with a healthy succession of visitors climbing the spiral staircase to view the coasts of South Wales and North Devon. The town's first lifeboat was provided in 1836 by the Corporation of Bridgwater.

In the 1920s, the High Light became the first in Britain to be automated, making the two keepers redundant. Their cottages were sold off as private dwellings.

The Low lighthouse was deactivated in 1969, but revived in 1993 after Trinity House closed the High Light because of the decline in shipping along the Parrett. Ships no longer dock at Bridgwater, but little Dunball Wharf north of the town still sees consignments of marine sand and gravels dredged from the Bristol Channel.

The High lighthouse was bought from Trinity House by a member of the Rothschild family in a sealed bid. Four years later it was again offered at auction, but failed to sell despite rumours that two celebrities were interested in it.

Dwarfed but still distinctive: the Low Light in the middle of the desert that is Burnham beach at low tide. It has been described as a 'bathing hut on stilts'. Steep Holm island, sister to Flat Holm, lies on the horizon.

The name of this house opposite Burnham's High Light invokes the third century BC Pharos of Alexandria, one of the Seven Wonders of the Ancient World. The term 'pharos' afterwards became applied to lighthouses everywhere.

Young journalist Patrick O'Hagan was sent by his editor to cover the story. He visited the lighthouse…and decided to buy it for himself.

Patrick has since converted it into luxury self-catering holiday accommodation, under the banner of Lighthouse Holidays. It sleeps six, but you must climb 120 steps to reach the Lantern Room. Needless to say, the views are unrivalled, and the sunsets are breathtaking. So while thanks to Davies, lighthouses made Burnham into a resort, the tallest of them all is now holiday accommodation.

Both lighthouses are painted white with a single vertical red stripe on the front face.

The Low lighthouse shows a white flash every 7.5 seconds, and a white, red or green directional light, depending on direction. It has a focal plane of 23ft.

The High Light technically remains in use, but only as a day range or daymark, that is, a lightless landmark to guide boats.

CHAPTER SIX
WATCHET HARBOUR

IN WATCHET, ALL ROADS lead to the harbour, and rightly so, because the sea has always been the life and soul of this attractive little Somerset port.

Watchet's early jetty was damaged in a storm in 1659. A more robust structure was constructed in the early eighteenth century with backing from local traders, and one of Watchet's biggest exports at this time was kelp, made from burned seaweed, for use in glassmaking. Trade was boosted by the arrival of Brunel's West Somerset Railway from Taunton, and the West Somerset Mineral Railway which brought iron ore down from the mines on the Brendon Hills for transhipment across the Bristol Channel for smelting at Ebbw Vale.

Around 1862, the east pier was built by the Bridgwater firm of Hennets. It included the harbour's most distinctive feature, the red cast-iron hexagonal harbour lighthouse.

Standing 22ft high with a white lantern, and green lens, it does not show a flashing light of the type associated with traditional lighthouses, as it is purely a harbour navigation mark, but displays a fixed green luminaire marking the starboard approach.

The harbour's commercial use ceased in 2001, and the following year it was taken over by Watchet Marina, which operates the lighthouse, and is nowadays packed with pleasure craft.

Watchet Harbour lighthouse dates from 1862. ROBIN JONES

The lighthouse stands at the end of the east pier, which acts as a breakwater. ROBIN JONES

CHAPTER SEVEN

LYNMOUTH FORELAND

BUILDING A LIGHTHOUSE on the highest point on land may seem an obvious idea, but it is not always the best.

The Bristol Channel is notorious for low cloud and fog, and in these conditions, a light may not be seen from such lofty heights.

In 1900, Trinity House added a further aid to navigation in the channel by constructing a lighthouse at Foreland Point, the northernmost point of the Exmoor coast, between Lynmouth and Porlock Weir, and where the cliffs soar to 990ft.

In this case, a daring site halfway down the cliffs was chosen, on the extremity of the

Lynmouth Foreland lighthouse, perched midway down an Exmoor cliff. JOHN LUCAS

Looking east past Foreland Point.
JOHN LUCAS

The tower of Foreland lighthouse.
TRINITY HOUSE

headland, cutting back into the rock face. The new Lynmouth Foreland lighthouse, also known as the Countisbury Forelands lighthouse, and its set of keepers' cottages, appear at first glance to be clinging precariously to the edge of the cliff, above the jagged rocks below and equally as far from the safety of the summit.

The 50ft tall lighthouse is a cylindrical brick tower with lantern and gallery attached to a keeper's cottage. It has a focal plane of 220ft.

The Fresnel lens shows four white flashes, separated by 2.2 seconds, every 15 seconds. The focal plane of the optic is 200ft above sea level.

The optic is a first order dioptric apparatus, with panels in two groups of four, revolving on a motor driven mercury float pedestal. It has a range of 18 nautical miles and an intensity of a million candela.

A private lighthouse access road leads from the A39 across the northern edge of Exmoor National Park and then descends down a series of breathtaking hairpin bends to the lighthouse and cottages.

However, most walkers view it from the South West Coast Path above. A cliff top walk from along the path leading from the Blue Ball Inn near Countisbury two miles away offers a winding but spectacular route 490ft above sea level around the cliff edges, offering magnificent channel views on a clear day. The upwards return journey is quite stiff.

The station was electrified in 1975 and automated in 1994. The foghorn is no longer in use. The National Trust now owns the cottage, along with much of the surrounding moorland, and rents it to holidaymakers. Ideal for walkers, birdwatchers and naturalists, on a clear day you have grandstand views of the channel stretching northwards to the Welsh coast and westwards to Lundy Island.

CHAPTER EIGHT
LYNMOUTH HARBOUR

The Rhenish Tower at Lynmouth, with its 'lighthouse' brazier on top. XLIBBER*

FOR YEARS, IT WAS ASSUMED that the trademark building of Lynmouth harbour, the square Rhenish Tower, with its brick turret carrying a brazier, was built as a lighthouse to warn passing ships off the rocky coastline.

Others now believe that it was not an official lighthouse, but a folly built in the 1850s by a General Rawdon, to store salt water for sea baths for visitors to his house, at a time when spa towns and 'taking the waters' were hugely popular amongst the well-to-do.

It was in the early nineteenth century that Lynmouth was "discovered" as a romantic location because of its mountain-like scenery. With the poets Robert Southey and Percy and Mary Shelley amongst its many admirers, it became known as "England's Little Switzerland". The tower was constructed in imitation of similar towers on the Rhine.

It was originally built without the distinctive machicolated balconies, but these were added at a later date to improve its image, because critics said the building was an eyesore.

Nevertheless, visitors and local residents alike eventually took it to their hearts.

The tower and around 100 other buildings and 28 bridges were washed away in the great freak storm of 15/16 August 1952 when the swollen River Lyn carved a trail of destruction through the village leaving 34 people dead.

The village was rebuilt and the Rhenish Tower, a listed building, was re-erected in 1954, retaining its original appearance.

Lynmouth's seafront is dominated by the Rhenish Tower. ROBIN JONES

CHAPTER NINE

ILFRACOMBE HARBOUR

WELCOME TO THE OLDEST working lighthouse in Britain – but it is far from what you might expect.

The tiny chapel of Chapel of St Nicholas on the top of steep Lantern Hill and watching over the harbour of Ilfracombe has been shining a light to guide mariners since at least 1650, while others say it dates back to the reign of Henry VIII or even before.

The natural layout of the safe haven on what can so often be a merciless coast made Ilfracombe the perfect place for a harbour to develop.

In medieval times, the town traded regularly with Ireland (Kinsale) and Tenby, and it

The little chapel lighthouse (left) stands like a guardian angel over Ilfracombe's harbour.
TOM PATTERSON

supplied men and ships to the English kings in time of conflict. In the eighteenth century, the town was home to many navy personnel. Until the railway transformed Ilfracombe into a resort in the nineteenth century, Ilfracombe lived off the sea, importing coal and lime from Wales, while maintaining a herring fishing fleet and boasting trade routes which ran as far as West Africa and the West Indies.

The chapel was originally a place of pilgrimage, with one bishop granting an indulgence of 40 days to anyone who visited it.

The 37ft purpose-built light tower was added by Trinity House in 1819, and has a focal plane of 127ft.

Local records show that between 1827 and 1849, the then lighthouse keeper John Davie and his wife John and Elizabeth had 14 children. The enterprising Elizabeth started a laundry to supplement the family income, and when John died in 1870, she took on the role of lighthouse keeper.

A green flash is shone every 2.5 seconds from the white lantern mounted on the top of the stone building, which is still open for worship. It has a range of six miles.

The current operator is North Devon District Council. The modern path to the chapel replaced a set of very steep steps to the right of the Pier Inn.

The chapel of St Nicholas with its tiny lighthouse tower and fish weathervane on top. ROB LAWSON/NORTH DEVON DISTRICT COUNCIL

CHAPTER TEN
BULL POINT

MORTE POINT, THE peninsula in north east Devon, has been described as "the place God made last and the devil will take first" because of the treacherous waters, jagged rocks and countless shipwrecks over the centuries.

Here, the devil not only took the ships but the lighthouse meant to save them. If you think the precarious position of Lynmouth Foreland lighthouse to be a little nerve jangling, that is nothing compared to what happened to the lighthouse here.

The name Morte Point literally means 'death point'. In the winter of 1852, five ships were wrecked.

One ship was wrecked carrying a cargo of live pigs, most of which survived, and reached dry land at a cove called – wait for it – Grunta Beach. Many will tell you that is why this little

The modern now-automated lighthouse at Bull Point. TRINITY HOUSE

The first Bull Point lighthouse in the early twentieth century. ROBIN JONES COLLECTION

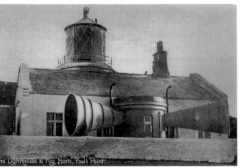

An Edwardian postcard shows the huge foghorn equipment originally fitted.
ROBIN JONES COLLECTION

The layout of the original lighthouse complex buildings. PHILIP HALLING*

cove was so named, but in reality the word was probably Scandinavian.

The village of Mortehoe was reputedly the haunt of wreckers and smugglers, groups who would find heaven on a coast that others considered hell. Folklore has it that wreckers had the practice of tying a lantern to a donkey's tail to simulate the sight of a ship moving at sea, and so give mariners a false idea of where they were, and so hit the rocks – a malignant lighthouse concept of folklore.

The Royal National Lifeboat Institution opened a lifeboat station at Morte Bay in 1871, but launching into the strong Atlantic winds blowing onto the west-facing beach proved problematic and so the station was closed in May 1900.

A 55ft tall lighthouse was constructed at Bull Point one-and-a-half miles away from Morte Point in 1879, after a contingent of ship owners, merchants, landowners and the local clergy appealed to Trinity House. In 1919, a foghorn was added and the lighthouse was electrified in 1960.

However, on 18 September 1972, the principal keeper noticed ground movement in the area of the engine room and the passage leading to the lighthouse, and reported fissures two inches wide to be opening up.

Early on Sunday 24 September, 50ft of the cliff face crashed into the sea. Another 50ft of the rock subsided leaving deep fissures inside the lighthouse boundary wall.

The fog signal station partly collapsed, disabling the siren.

Trinity House called on the Nature Conservancy Council to return a skeletal light tower previously sited at Braunton Sands and which had been given to the group when declared redundant.

That light tower was moved to Bull Point and the optic from the damaged lighthouse was installed on it, while a temporary hut housed the fog signals.

A new lighthouse was built between 1974-6 at a cost of £71,000, it was designed so that all the equipment from 1960 could be 'recycled' and reused inside it, including the optic. The old lighthouse was demolished.

The new 35ft tall lighthouse, which comprised a modern cylindrical brick tower with lantern and gallery attached to a square single-storey building, and has a focal plane of 177ft, was automated in 1995, the fog signal having been discontinued in 1988.

Three white flashes are shown every 10 seconds plus also a continuous red hazard light westward over Rockham Shoal. It has a light intensity of 800,000 candela and, standing 177ft above mean water level, can be seen for 24 nautical miles.

The keepers' cottages are now hired out as holiday accommodation.

CHAPTER ELEVEN
LUNDY ISLAND

IN THE WORLD OF UK lighthouses, Lundy Island is as high as you can get.

Work on building the first, the Old Light which dominates the centre of the island, began in 1787 when the first foundations were laid, but it was not until Trinity House obtained a 999-year lease in 1819 that it was completed.

Standing at 407ft above sea level, the base of the Old Light on the summit of Chapel Hill is higher than that of any other lighthouse in Britain. The tower itself stands at 97ft.

It was designed by engineer Daniel Asher Alexander, whose other works included the lighthouse towers at Harwich. The builder was Joseph Nelson while the superintendent of works was James Turnbull.

Two lights were shown from the tower, the lower a fixed white light and the upper a white light which flashed every 60 seconds. At this time, such an innovation was cutting-edge technology as far as navigation aids was concerned.

However, the Old Light was not one of Alexander's better ideas. The height of the light reduced its value in fog, necessitating a separate fog signal battery to be built in 1869.

Furthermore, the pair of lights revolved so fast that they gave the misleading impression to ships more than five miles away that it was a single fixed light with no flashes. That factor may have contributed to the wreck of the *La Jeune Emma* at Cefn Sidan beach in Carmarthenshire in 1828, whose crew, it was said, mistook the Lundy light for that of Ushant in thick fog. Among the 13 who drowned was Adeline Coquelin, the 12 year-old niece of Napoleon Bonaparte's divorced wife Josephine.

Lundy lies in the centre of the entrance to the Bristol Channel, and the rocks around its coast have always presented a danger to shipping. Yet ships could not avoid sailing close to the island, because of the treacherous shingle banks in the fast-flowing Bristol Channel.

However, lying 12 miles off the coast of north Devon, it has been an extremely difficult place for the mainland authorities to control. Indeed, at several points in history, this superb natural fortress made it a haven for pirates, including its infamous thirteenth-century owner William de Marisco, who would almost certainly have welcomed the rich pickings from passing ships striking the rocks below.

The blatant disregard for the law long associated with Lundy took a different twist in the case of Barnstaple MP Thomas Benson, the Sheriff of Devon. He leased the island and used it

The granite tower of Lundy's Old lighthouse. ROBIN JONES

Lundy North lighthouse, which works in tandem with the one on Caldey Island. STEVE HODGSON*

to house convicts who he had been paid to transport to Virginia, making them his personal slaves on Lundy.

Benson also masterminded an insurance fraud in which his convicts unloaded a valuable cargo of pewter and linen and concealed it in an island cave, before setting fire to the ship and claiming that the goods had been lost. The roguish Benson eventually fled to Portugal where he died.

The Old lighthouse was accessed from the island's main landing beach by a road built by Jamaica sugar plantation magnate William Hudson Heaven, who bought Lundy for £9,870 in 1834. He declared it a free island, successfully placing it outside the jurisdiction of mainland magistrates. He also built much of the island village, while his son the Reverend Hudson Grosset Heaven added St Helena's church in 1896.

The first lighthouse was abandoned in 1897, when Trinity House built two replacements at each end of the island, the white-painted North and South lighthouses.

The 55ft tall northern light was built on a narrow plateau amidst large shrieking colonies of herring gulls, guillemots and razorbills.

Its light was originally produced by a 75mm petroleum vapour burner when electricity was installed. Oil supplies were lifted up to the lighthouse from a small quay below using a sled, and then hauled to the tower along a narrow gauge railway.

Lundy largely comprises a windswept plateau atop 400ft cliffs. ROBIN JONES

Lundy North lighthouse all but balanced on a knife edge.
TRINITY HOUSE

Several lighthouses had similar private railways, mostly, as in this case, using winch and cable haulage. The railway can still be seen today, although it has not been used since 1971, when the lighthouse was converted to electricity, the discharge bulb fed from the mains supply to the island.

The North lighthouse was intended to aid coastal shipping trading limestone and coal to central and north Wales, while ensuring traffic from North America avoided confusing the Bristol and English channels. It operates in conjunction with the lighthouse on Caldey Island in Pembrokeshire.

Lundy South lighthouse and the landing beach, where visitors arrive.
TRINITY HOUSE

On 30 May 1906, the keeper was surprised to encounter a landing party from the Royal Navy battleship *HMS Montagu*, which had run aground in heavy fog near Shutter Rock on the island's south-west corner. The crew thought they were at Hartland Point on the mainland and argued with the keeper for some time before finally accepting he knew which lighthouse he kept.

The Royal Navy, which sacked the captain and navigating officer, sold her for scrap in 1907. It took 15 years for her to be dismantled, and live ammunition shells still lie on the seabed.

Lundy North was automated in 1985 and modernised in 1991 when it was converted to solar power with a new Orga lantern installed on the disued fog signal building. With an intensity of 11,740 candela, it has a focal plane of 157ft and gives a quick white flash every 15 seconds which can be seen for 17 nautical miles.

Lundy South lighthouse stands above the island's main landing beach. It comprises a 52ft squat cylindrical brick tower with lantern and gallery attached to a pair of keepers' houses and has a focal plane of 175ft. It was automated in 1994 when it was converted to solar power.

With an intensity of 11,100 candela, it emits a white flash every five seconds, and with a range of 15 nautical miles, can be glimpsed off the north Devon coast. The fog signal, which is mounted on top of the lantern, emits a two-second blast every 25 seconds.

Further attempts to keep Lundy as a realm unto itself outside English law were made in the twentieth century, by businessman Martin Coles Harman, who bought the island in 1924. Just like Marisco centuries before, Harman became 'king of Lundy', and in 1929 even issued his own currency, the puffin and half puffin, claiming that the island was a self-governing dominion.

For this, he was convicted under the 1870 Coinage Act and compelled to withdraw the coins. However, he was allowed to issue his own island stamps, after the Post Office decided in 1927 to stop serving its declining population, which now stands at 28.

The island is now owned by the National Trust, but leased to the Landmark Trust.

In the summer months, it can be visited on day trips aboard the trust's ferry MS *Oldenburg* from Ilfracombe or Bideford.

Lundy today has 23 holiday properties, including the two keepers' flats at the Old Light, and the one-person Old Light Cottage which was the keepers' store. Unlike the Trinity House pair, the Old Light can be visited.

The railway which took supplies to Lundy North lighthouse from the little quay below. IAN DINMORE

The top of Lundy South lighthouse. ADRIAN BOLISTON*

The legendary Lundy one puffin coin of 1929. ROBIN JONES COLLECTION

CHAPTER TWELVE
TAW AND TORRIDGE

THE NEAREST YOU WILL get to a desert in England is Braunton Burrows in North Devon, which comprises the country's biggest sand dune system. A Site of Special Scientific Interest, it is fronted by the great three-mile expanse of Saunton Sands.

The dune system ends where the River Taw flowing from the east meets the Torridge coming up from the south, before flowing out to sea together via Bideford Bar, the dangerous sandbank which crossed the mouth of the combined estuary.

At this southernmost extremity of Devon's mini-desert, there used to be two lights, a high lighthouse and a smaller low one.

The high light was an 86ft white-painted close-boarded wooden octagonal tower structure with wooden braces to support the outside, and was built in 1920 by Joseph Nelson, who built the Burnham-on-Sea high and low lights. It had a red stripe and a traditional light, with square living quarters on the side. It had a range of 14 miles.

The long-gone Braunton lighthouse.
ROBIN JONES COLLECTION

Around 300 yards away over the dunes was a low light, a 15ft-high wooden hut with a red stripe and a window light supported on wooden legs.

Next to the low light stood a large mast and ball, while out in the estuary, a marker comprising a horizontal board fixed to two posts indicated the halfway stage between high and low tides.

When the tide reached the bottom of the board it was either half flood or half ebb. The keeper of the high light kept an eye on this during daylight and when the tide reached the bottom of the board, the high light keeper walked over to the low light and raised the ball to display whether the tide was halfway coming in or halfway going out, the purpose being to let sailors know if it was safe to tackle Bideford Bar.

A lifeboat station was opened on Braunton Burrows in 1848, taking its crew from the Appledore station on the opposite side of the Torridge. It was closed in 1918 due to a shortage of manpower after World War One.

Despite their name, the Braunton lighthouses stood three miles away from the village, a major drawback in the early days when there were no surfaced roads across the dunes. The two keepers and their families therefore used Appledore instead for provisions and facilities. Fresh water was supplied by boat, to supplement the rainwater collected in butts, along with coal supplies.

The keepers took it in turns to work four or eight-hour shifts, which meant that neither could ever travel far from home, and they must have often wondered whether it was worth

Crow Point light at low tide. BRIAN PIBWORTH

Above left: *Instow Front Range light.*
TRINITY HOUSE

Above centre: *Instow Rear Range light.* DEREK HARPER*

Above right: *The modern light at Crow Point.* SHARON STRETTON

making the arduous journeys across the dunes for such a short spell away.

Modifications to the high light were made in 1889 and to the low light in 1902.

The shifting sands eventually rendered the high light unstable and the keepers were withdrawn in 1945, and after being declared redundant, both lights were demolished in 1957.

The remains of the high light stand about half a mile away from the replacement modern utilitarian light tower at Crow Point, a 25ft tubular steel skeletal structure with a range of five miles built on a sandy spit just inside the entrance to the Taw opposite Instow. Operated by Trinity House, it has a focal plane of 27ft and flashes every five seconds, red or white, depending on direction.

Torridge District Council, operator of the Port of Bideford, has two lighthouses at Instow to guide ships through the narrow channel into the Taw.

The Instow Range Front lighthouse is situated on the west bank of the Taw on the north side of the village. The 59ft white square steel skeletal tower has a gallery and a rectangular vertically-slatted daymark. It has a focal plane of 72ft and its white light flashes for five seconds on and one second off, and has a range of 18 miles.

The smaller Instow Range Rear light is sited a quarter of a mile away, on a hillside pasture off Rectory Lane. Painted white, it comprises a 28ft post light mounted on top of a single-storey hut, with a focal plane of 126ft. Its white light flashes 7.5 seconds on, 2.5 seconds off, and has a range of 8½ miles.

CHAPTER THIRTEEN
HARTLAND POINT

HARTLAND POINT WAS KNOWN to the Romans as Herculis Promontorium, the 'promontory of Hercules', because of the furious tidal conditions where the Bristol Channel coast turns to meet the full force of the Atlantic surge.

Like Morte Point, Hartland Point, a 325ft rocky outcrop of land on the north-westernmost tip of Devon, has seen countless shipwrecks, the earliest being recorded in the fourteenth century.

Trinity House ordered a lighthouse to be erected on the headland in 1874, and chose James Douglass, best known for designing the fourth Eddystone lighthouse, to build it.

Douglass, born in 1826 in Bow, London, the eldest son of civil engineer Nicholas Douglass, joined the engineering department of Trinity House. He and his brother William assisted their father during the construction of Bishop Rock lighthouse.

Later, Trinity House asked him to design Pembrokeshire's Smalls lighthouse, which he based on John Smeaton's third Eddystone lighthouse, using dovetailed granite blocks for added strength.

Douglass then designed Wolf Rock lighthouse and in 1862 became engineer in chief of Trinity House, for which he designed 20 lighthouses, including Hartland Point.

The finished lighthouse was blessed by Frederick Temple, Bishop of Exeter, who later

The view from the lighthouse gallery, which is now closed to visitors.
ROBIN JONES

The lighthouse as seen from the south.
DAVID SPENDER*

An aerial view of Hartland Point lighthouse. TRINITY HOUSE

became Archbishop of Canterbury.

Built on a large rock at the tip of the point, rather than on top of the headland, the lighthouse has always faced being undermined by the sea. Remedial action was taken at regular intervals by breaking rock from the cliffs to fall on the beach and form a barrier against the waves. Every time a north-westerly gale coincided with a high spring tide, these rock deposits were washed away.

The ultimate solution was to build a permanent barrier, and a sea wall 20ft high and 98ft long appeared in 1925. Two years later, the lighthouse was electrified.

Hartland Point lighthouse was manned by four keepers who lived in attached cottages with their families. These dwellings were pulled down when the lighthouse was automated in 1984, to make way for a helipad, because the access road is also vulnerable to rock falls and landslips.

The Grade 2 listed white-painted brick circular tower is 59ft tall with the lamp being 121ft above mean sea level. The light, a white group flashing six times every 15 seconds, has a range of 25 miles. The foghorn emits a five-second blast every 60 seconds.

Hartland Point has continued to claim ships even in modern times. The Dutch-owned *MS Johanna*, carrying wheat from the Netherlands to Cardiff, went aground on rocks 400 yards from the lighthouse during bad weather on 31 December 1982. Four crew members were rescued by a helicopter from RAF Chivenor while three officers were taken off by the Clovelly lifeboat.

The rusting remains of the hull lie on the stony beach below the lighthouse: while humans can be warned off by lighthouses, Mother Nature cannot be tamed, as can still be seen.

It may not be the sea that will finally stop the lighthouse working, but advancements in high-tech navigational aids. In its 2010 Aids to Navigation Review, Trinity House proposed to shut Hartland Point and several others on the grounds that Global Positioning Systems have superseded them. However, after protests it agreed to continue the light but at reduced power.

The Ministry of Defence has a radar station on the point, controlled from nearby RAF Hartland Point, and used for air traffic control of both military and civilian aircraft. The unusual white-dome-topped building can be sighted from up to 10 miles away.

An unmanned coastguard station stands near the lighthouse.

Hartland had its own harbour, Hartland Quay, to the south of the point. Built in the late sixteenth century, most of it was swept away in 1887 and the last commercial cargo was landed six years later. Here, the sea will never give up.

The remains of the MS Johanna *seen from the lighthouse.* RICHARD GREEENWOOD*

The Hartland Point radar station is also a landmark. RCOH*

47

CHAPTER FOURTEEN
PADSTOW AND THE DOOM BAR

AS FAR AS SHIPWRECKS and dangers to navigation are concerned, the most dangerous stretch of English coastal waters is the Goodwin Sands off Kent. Following behind is the great sandbank across the mouth of the Camel estuary in North Cornwall, known as the Doom Bar.

The word actually derives from 'dune bar' – before 1900, it was known as Dunbar Sands - but Doom Bar is more than appropriate, in terms of the huge loss of life it has caused over the centuries, including around 600 wrecks since records began about 200 years ago.

The Stepper Point daymark guards the entrance to the Camel estuary.

A sand dredger returning to Padstow harbour from the Doom Bar. ROBIN JONES

The seaward view from inside the daymark. ROBIN JONES

A popular legend relates that a mermaid killed by a Padstow fisherman after he mistook her for a seal cursed the port, causing the estuary to refill with sand again as soon as it was dredged. Indeed, at very low tides, it is almost possible to walk across the vast expanse of sandbanks from Padstow to Rock.

Said to have first appeared during the reign of Henry VIII, the Doom Bar became so notorious that many vessels would rather face being wrecked on the coast than negotiate the Doom Bar, in defiance of the old saying "from Padstow Point to Lundy Light, is a sailor's grave by day or night."

Traders took several measures in a bid to reduce the danger. In the early nineteenth century, a hollow stone rubble-built circular tower, a daymark, was erected at Stepper Point, the 242ft headland to the west of the Doom Bar, as a guide to mariners entering the estuary. Originally washed with lime, it is now a listed building.

Even more extreme measures were taken to combat the menace of the Doom Bar, including the cutting away of a huge section of cliff below the daymark in the late 1850s.

It appeared that the danger was at its worst when westerly winds swirling around Stepper Point, known as "the flaws", set up a treacherous cross wind and eddies; any ships trying to sail past were blown over the Doom Bar, where the waters are deceptively shallow, and wrecked. By quarrying away part of the point, the swirls and eddies could be deflected, it was thought.

The remains of three large capstans can be seen by the quarries. If a ship got into difficulties, a pilot gig and crew set out with hawsers, tied them to the ship, which was then winched in using the capstans.

Another scheme, which did not come to fruition, came from the Plymouth & Padstow

Sharp's Brewery of Rock opposite Padstow produces the award-winning Doom Bar ale. SHARP BREWERY

Railway Company, which proposed building a breakwater on the Doom Bar itself, preventing the build up of sand in the estuary and boosting the trade of Padstow, a port famous for its 'Obby 'Oss celebrations on 1 May.

On 15 September 1816, HMS *Whiting*, a 12-gun schooner captured in 1812 during Britain's short war with the United States, became the only naval vessel to be grounded on the Doom Bar. Lieutenant John Jackson, the officer in charge, was court-martialled and lost one year's seniority for negligence, while three crewmen received 50 lashes for desertion.

The biggest wreck on the Doom Bar was the barque *Antoinette*, which floundered on 1 January 1895 with Welsh coal destined for Brazil. Because the wreck presented an additional danger to shipping, it was gelignited. The explosion was so loud that it was said to have shattered every window in Padstow.

So feared was the Doom Bar that when the brigantine *Angele* floundered there on 12 November 1911, the Padstow lifeboat crew refused to go out, and the coxswain had to raise a replacement from surrounding villages.

Today, the dreaded sandbank is much easier to negotiate because of constant dredging, and it is also a location for wreck diving.

Nearby the daymark, there is a white light flashing every ten seconds, with a visibility of four miles. At St Saviour's Point nearer Padstow, a green secondary light flashes every ten seconds. The entrance to the harbour is marked by two fixed green secondary lights on the north side and two red ones, also vertical, on the south. The red painted cast iron 20ft column with a ladder attached on the south pier head and topped with a modern navigational red lamp was installed in 1868.

The 'cut away' headland designed to reduce the danger presented by winds blowing ships on to the Doom Bar. ROBIN JONES

CHAPTER FIFTEEN
TREVOSE HEAD

IN 1809 A LIGHTHOUSE was first proposed for the Padstow area, as there was no navigational aid in the Bristol Channel other than the old Lundy light to the north and the Longships to the south.

The demands were stepped up in 1811 when the *Bloodhound* was wrecked at Harlyn Bay. Trinity House looked again at the situation in 1813 to no avail, and again in 1832. It was not until 1 December 1847 that a light was shone from the towering granite headland of Trevose Head. The 88ft tall lighthouse, the last to be run on compressed air and paraffin, was built by Thomas and Jacob Olver of Falmouth, a firm of public works contractors.

At first, there were two fixed lights on the headland, the present-day high light 204ft above sea level and a lower light 50ft in front of it, 129ft above sea level. Initially, illumination was provided by an oil light comprising wicks backed with reflectors.

The lantern is 204ft above sea level.
ROBIN JONES

The oversize fog signal equipment installed in 1912. ROBIN JONES
COLLECTION

Trevose Head lighthouse and keepers' cottages. TRINITY HOUSE

Trevose Head lighthouse stands sentinel over a treacherous coast. ROBIN JONES

Far left: *After sunset at Trevose Head.*
TRINITY HOUSE

Left: *Bull Rock and the Quies as seen from the lighthouse.* ROBIN JONES

Surprisingly, for an area plagued by sea mists which obscure lights, a fog signal was not installed until 1882.

That year, an occulting light was fixed in the high light, and the lower light was discontinued. Three keepers were appointed to man the station. The fog signal was visibly upgraded in 1912, with new apparatus looking like the bellows of a giant folding camera being installed. It was designed by Lord Rayleigh, and comprised a huge trumpet 36ft long with an 18ft by 2ft aperture for the purpose of producing a wide horizontal spread of sound.

On 6 February 1913 the new fog signal entered service at an inauguration ceremony.

Anachronistic as it looks today, it was so successful that it remained in service until 1963, when it was replaced by a Supertyphon with eight horns. Also, in 1912, the light was modified, with a new catadioptric lens powered by a clockwork motor driven by weights. A Hood vapour burner was installed in 1920, making another great improvement.

The lighthouse, which has a focal plane of 204ft, was electrified in 1974 and automated in 1995.

The modern-day light emits one white flash every 7.5 seconds, with an intensity of 89,900 candela and a range of 20 nautical miles. The light is controlled by a photocell mounted on the lantern murette, while a Tideland ML300 lantern mounted on the lantern gallery handrail gives an emergency light visible for 20 nautical miles.

The fog signal, now an electric omnidirectional signal controlled by a fog detector, gives two blasts every 30 seconds.

The lighthouse is reached by a private road which passes the entrance to the modern Padstow lifeboat station, which was moved to Mother Ivey's Bay in 1967 from Hawker's Cove because of the silting around the Doom Bar.

Many people drive to the lighthouse to watch the glorious sunsets, which are highly prized by photographers. From the adjoining headland, it can be seen that the shark's fin-shaped Bull Rock lines up with the unalike twin rocks of the Quies out to sea, indicating that the coastline long ago extended much further out before wave erosion took its toll.

Climbing to the top inside Trevose Head lighthouse. ROBIN JONES

CHAPTER SIXTEEN
NEWQUAY HUER'S HUT

NEWQUAY'S DISTINCTIVE SMALL, round huer's hut has for centuries been one of the town's best-known buildings: indeed, its shape and coat of gleaming whitewash suggests that it has been moved straight from the Greek Cyclades to North Cornwall.

Nobody knows exactly when this Grade 2 listed rubblestone building with its prominent square chimney and narrow stairway leading to its flat roof was built, and it may have originally served as a hermitage for a holy man.

According to a plaque mounted outside, the hut may have been used as a primitive lighthouse around this time.

From about the fourteenth century, however, it became the home of the town 'huer', a man whose job it was to scan the oceans for signs of incoming pilchard shoals, and then shout the alert to waiting fishermen: "hevva hevva" (Cornish for 'here they are'). Townsfolk would then drop everything and rush out to sea in their boats, nets at the ready.

Lights might also have been displayed from the hut at this time, to guide the fishing boats back into the town harbour below.

Visible for miles down the coast, the white hut doubled up as a two-way daymark. The huer would direct the movement of the boats at sea, standing on the roof using semaphore-like signals made by waving two small furze bushes covered with cloth. It is said that this system was also used to pass news to local sailors, such as the birth of a child to their wives!

The novelist Wilkie Collins, author of *The Woman in White*, described the sight of a huer at work in his 1851 collection of travel essays entitled *Rambles Beyond Railways*. He related that a visitor "would see a man standing on the extreme edge of a precipice, just over the sea, gesticulating in a very remarkable manner, with a bush in his hand…in short, apparently acting the part of a maniac of the most dangerous character."

Huers needed to concentrate hard on their job, for their town's livelihood depended on him. One story relates that a notice above the fireplace in a similar hut at St Ives banned playing cards.

The phrase "food, money, light, and all in one night" described a catch, because pilchards provided all this, their oil sent to cities for use in early street lighting. The whole town would celebrate, and local women baked 'hevva cakes'.

The pilchard shoals disappeared from Cornish waters in the nineteenth century, and the huer's job was finally done.

Incidentally, Newquay's new four-screen cinema which opened in spring 2011 is called the Lighthouse Cinema, because of the panoramic view from the top projection level of the building across Newquay Bay to Trevose Head lighthouse.

The huer's hut overlooking the surfing beaches of Newquay. PENGANNEL*

CHAPTER SEVENTEEN
PORTREATH

THE HEYDAY OF PORTREATH was also that of Cornwall's mining industry. Before the nineteenth century, it was a small fishing village, its name deriving from the Cornish for 'sandy cove'.

Its first quay was built in 1713 near Amy's Point, and was accessed by a mule track down the cliffs, but was destroyed by heavy seas sometime before 1749.

Portreath took off in 1760 when the existing pier was built, providing a sheltered berth for small sailing vessels to load copper ore. Harbours were vital for the burgeoning mining industry that sprang up at the hinterland of Camborne and Redruth, a major heartland of the Industrial Revolution. From Portreath, copper ore was despatched to Swansea, with the ships bringing back steam coal for the giant beam engines powering the Cornish mines.

Demand for coal increased and led to the harbour being enlarged in 1801, with the new outer basin accommodating 25 ships, which became known as the Welsh Fleet.

A seine fishing company was established in 1800, fishing mostly for pilchards.

In 1809, local landowners and mine owners pooled their resources to build Cornwall's first railway, a private horse-drawn plateway between Portreath and Poldice, to carry ore to the harbour and coal back to the mines, replacing the inadequate and often-muddy mule paths. By 1819, it linked the St Day mines to the harbour, and was superseded by the Portreath branch line of the Hayle Railway which connected the important Camborne and Pool mines with Portreath, which it reached down a massive incline, the ruins of which dominate the little port today.

The railway helped Portreath take off big time. Trade peaked around 1840, when 100,000 tons of copper ore were shipped.

The collapse of the copper trade and the drifting away of the pilchard shoals led to the harbour, hitherto a private port owned by the Bassett family of nearby Tehidy, becoming a free port. In the 1960s, the harbour stopped trading commercially, and passed into local authority ownership.

Tourism took off at Portreath, although much of the harbour became derelict and fenced off. However, it gradually became refilled with pleasure craft and inshore fishing boats. The old mineral railway network has been turned into a coast-to-coast cyclepath from Portreath Harbour to Devoran.

Waves breaking over the squat Portreath lighthouse. DAVE TASKIS*

The pier has the remains of one of the West Country's 'forgotten' lighthouses. Standing at the end of the disused tram line, it comprises a stumpy stone circular tower with a flat stepped roof, capped with a pinnacle that once held a navigation light.

On top of the cliffs to the east of the harbour stands a 25ft-high stone conical daymark. The white-painted tower has a small door in the base.

Also, there is a small pilchard lookout hut on the harbour edge and a further brick castellated lookout tower near the daymark.

Furthermore, a light was shone from a mining stack on the hill of Carn Brea between Redruth and Camborne in 1815, to act as a guide for passing boats at sea. However, this practice had ceased by the 1880s when the stack was partially demolished.

Portreath harbour, showing the pier with the tiny lighthouse at the end, and the daymark on the cliffs above.
ROBIN JONES

CHAPTER EIGHTEEN
GODREVY ISLAND

BEAUTIFUL GODREVY ISLAND and its lighthouse have long provided inspiration to the artists' 'colony' of St Ives. However, it is in the world of literature rather than the visual arts that it is best known.

The tower is said to have been the inspiration for Virginia Woolf's classic 1927 modernist novel *To The Lighthouse*.

The novel is set in the Isle of Skye, but Woolf spent many childhood holidays in the St Ives locality, and transferred several of its geographical features to the west coast of Scotland. Indeed, there are many similarities between the plot and her own life.

Aerial view of Godrevy Island, with its walled enclosure surrounding James Walker's lighthouse. TRINITY HOUSE

The island viewed from near Godrevy Point. ROBIN JONES

The cover of the first edition of Virginia Woolf's To The Lighthouse.

In one instance, Woolf's brother Adrian was not allowed to go on an expedition to Godrevy lighthouse, while in the novel, James Ramsey looks forward to visiting the Scottish lighthouse only for the trip to be cancelled. It is only at the end of the novel that the characters achieve their ambition of visiting the lighthouse.

The novel includes the lines: "Turning, she looked across the bay. And there, sure enough, coming regularly across the waves, first two quick strokes and then one long steady stroke, was the light of the lighthouse. It had been lit."

In 1882, shortly after the novelist's birth, her father started renting Talland House in St Ives and it was used by the family for long summer holidays during the next decade. The house, its setting and the St Ives Bay seascape formed the basis for the fictional landscape in Skye.

To The Lighthouse has been named by *TIME* magazine as one of the top 100 novels between 1923 and the present day.

The home of sea birds like gulls and oystercatchers, Godrevy Island stands off Godrevy Point, on the far eastern side of the bay, of which it is the most striking feature. However, what the visitor, or the sailor for that matter, does not as readily see is the treacherous reef called the

Close-up view of the lighthouse today, with its solar panels to the left. TIM GREEN*

Stones which extends outwards towards St Ives.

Many ships had been lost on this reef before 30 November 1854, when the iron screw steamer *Nile* was wrecked with the loss of all 60 passengers and crew.

A public outcry led to Trinity House building a lighthouse on the island.

Its designer, engineer James Walker, was born in Falkirk in 1781 and became apprenticed to his uncle Ralph Walker. Under him, James gained experience in the design and construction of London's West India and East India Docks. Around 1810, he began work on the Surrey Commercial Docks and remained its engineer until his death in 1862. He became president of the Institution of Civil Engineers from 1834-45, succeeding the great bridge and canal builder Thomas Telford.

The 86ft white octagonal cylindrical tower, which has a focal plane of 120ft, and its adjoining keepers' cottages were constructed from rubble stone bedded in mortar. Planning began in 1859 with building starting the following year. The total project cost £7,082 15s 7d, and the first light was shone on 1 March 1859.

The original revolving optic was driven by a clockwork motor, which in turn was powered by a large weight running down a cavity in the tower wall.

At first, two keepers were appointed to maintain the pair of lights, one a bright flashing white every 10 seconds, and the other fixed red and shown to the north west, warning ships away from the Stones.

The station also had a fog signal bell weighing 300cwt which sounded once every five seconds.

Just before 1900, a telephone link with the mainland was installed.

The lighthouse became automated as early as 1939, after it was decided that because of the decline in local shipping a manned station was no longer necessary. A new fixed catadioptric lens illuminated by an acetylene burner was installed in place of the original, while the fog bell was taken out, and the keepers moved off the island.

In 1995, modernisation saw the Grade 2 listed lighthouse converted to solar power.

Today, the 75-watt tungsten halogen lamp emits one white and one red flash every ten seconds. The white light has an intensity of 4,370 candela with a range of 12 nautical miles and the red one 817 candela with a range of nine nautical miles. The keeper's houses have been demolished, although the ruins can be made out.

In 2010, Trinity House considered closing the lighthouse, claiming it had been rendered obsolete by high-tech navigational technology, and cost £108,000 a year to operate. However, local campaigners, especially Woolf fans, mounted a campaign to keep Godrevy flashing.

Trinity House backtracked after concluding that the lighthouse was still the most effective means of local navigation, but its range was to be reduced from 12 to ten nautical miles.

It is little wonder why so many artists come to the sweeping whitesand beaches of Gwithian and Godrevy Towans to paint the island, with its dazzling splash of springtime colour with primroses, sea thrift and heather surrounded by the Atlantic breakers so beloved of local surfers if not seamen.

The lighthouse tower today.
TRINITY HOUSE

A set of circular furniture from Godrevy lighthouse has been displayed inside the award-winning National Maritime Museum Cornwall in Falmouth. NATIONAL MARITIME MUSEUM CORNWALL

CHAPTER NINETEEN
ST IVES HARBOUR

GENERATIONS OF ARTISTS have venerated St Ives for having one of the most beautiful harbours anywhere, and the huge numbers of galleries in the town are testament to the fact that it has long been a magnet for the creative, drawn by the 'perfect' light falling on the whitesand beaches and azure sea.

Before the railway line from St Erth opened in 1877 and brought tourists flocking to St Ives, it had long been the most important pilchard fishing port on Cornwall's north coast of. It remains in constant use today by fishing boats, pleasure cruisers and other leisure craft.

In echoes of the Ilfracombe lighthouse, a beacon at the chapel of St Nicholas at St Ives was recorded in 1538.

In our anti-clockwise journey around the coast, we have yet to meet John Smeaton: he was

The prefabricated lighthouse of 1890.
ROBIN JONES

The original harbour lighthouse pictured in the early twentieth century.
ROBIN JONES COLLECTION

the architect of the third Eddystone lighthouse described in Chapter 37. However, one of his lesser-known designs, the south pier at St Ives, also known as Smeaton's Pier, was his first harbour construction. It was constructed by Thomas Richardson, who had been Smeaton's foreman mason at Eddystone.

The rubble and masonry pier was built in 1766, utilising an ingenious design with a reservoir on the seabed that fills at high tide, allowing wave action to scour the harbour and prevent anything like the extent of silting we saw at Padstow. Originally 360ft long, 35,000 tons of stone were used in its construction. The pier, which is 24ft across, was extended by a further 300ft in the 1890s.

The older of the two lighthouses was not built by Smeaton, despite a popular misconception. The 20ft square cylindrical stone tower, which has an eight-sided gallery and

Beautiful St Ives harbour at low tide with Smeaton's Pier and the 1890 lighthouse in the background.
ROBIN JONES

a broad observation room instead of a traditional lantern, was constructed by James and Edward Harvey in 1831, on top of Smeaton's original harbour wall.

It was taken out of use as early as 1890, when the pier was extended, and afterwards used as a storeroom. In 1996, it was badly damaged by fire, but subsequently restored.

In 1890, it was replaced by a new 32ft tower on the far end of the pier. This cast iron tower with its lantern and gallery was prefabricated in Bath by Stothert and Pitt Ltd.

The lantern from a post light that had been fixed nearby in the late 1860s is now in the St Ives Museum. The white-painted lighthouse operated by Cornwall Council has a focal plane of 27ft and displays two continuous green lights, one above the other. There is a corresponding secondary light post on the West Pier opposite, showing two red lights. Both are visible for three miles.

A section of a Great Western Railway travel poster of St Ives depicting the lighthouse. ROBIN JONES

CHAPTER TWENTY
PENDEEN

THE COAST OF PENWITH, the westernmost part of Cornwall, has been a graveyard for ships for centuries. Gurnard's Head a prominent headland on the north coast of this peninsula, has been responsible for more than its fair share of maritime calamities.

The danger here was that passing ships struggled to catch sight of either Trevose Head to the east or Longships lighthouse to the west, because of the high cliffs. Unable to work out their positions, they became lost, and the hidden rocks near Pendeen Watch gave no quarter.

In 1891, Trinity House finally decided to build a lighthouse and fog signal at Pendeen.

The buildings were designed by Trinity House engineer Sir Thomas Matthews, with Arthur Carkeek of Redruth the builder and Chance Brothers providing the lantern. First of all, the headland needed to be flattened to make way for the complex of buildings that would sit on top of it. The job involved the building of a massive retaining wall on the seaward side. It was not until 26 September 1900 that the light was shone for the first time.

The lighthouse and its keepers' cottages.
TRINITY HOUSE

The 55ft tall concrete-clad rubblestone tower comprises two rooms, one above the other, with the lantern on top and the machinery is built into the base of the tower. At first, oil was pumped to the Argand lamp from the room below, but the lighthouse was electrified in 1926.

An apparatus containing the lenses revolves around the lamp. The optic weighs two-and-a-half tons, floating in a trough containing three-quarters-of-a-ton of mercury which means it can be moved by the slenderest of touches. The light is 194ft above water level and comprises a white group flashing four times every 15 seconds. With an intensity of 150,000 candela, its range is 16 nautical miles.

The fog signal, based in a separate building, sounds once every 20 seconds.

An E-shaped building is divided into four cottages, three used by the keepers' families and the fourth as an office. Behind the cottages were three kitchen gardens, which proved useless because of the exposed position of the lighthouse. At first, rainwater was collected off the flat roof of the accommodation block and stored in an underground tank to serve the cottages.

The lighthouse was automated in 1995 with the keepers moving out on 3 May. The original Fresnel lens is still in use, but a new lamp plinth with a two-position lamp changer was fitted along with an emergency light and a new fog signal complete with automatic fog detector.

In February 2010, Pendeen was listed among the ten best lighthouses in which to stay in Britain, along with Burnham-on-Sea's High light. The two-bedroom keeper's accommodation, Argus Cottage sleeps three, and has earplugs provided for when the foghorn sounds.

Below the lighthouse can be found the wreck of another ship, the *Liberty*, parts of which are still visible at low tide on Liberty Rock.

The lighthouse and its keepers' cottages.
TRINITY HOUSE

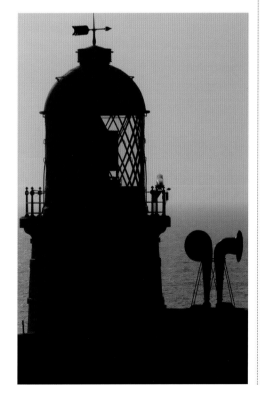

Opposite: *An aerial view of the Pendeen lighthouse complex.* TRINITY HOUSE

The tower and foghorn in silhouette.
MARTIN HARTLAND*

CHAPTER TWENTY ONE
CHAPEL CARN BREA

THE FIRST AND LAST hill in Britain. That is a traditional description given to Chapel Carn Brea, a 657ft granite outcrop three miles from St Just-in-Penwith and overlooking Sennen Cove and the Atlantic two miles away.

The hilltop, owned by the National Trust, is famous for its late neolithic and early Bronze Age burial chambers. It also has the remains of the thirteenth-century chapel of St Michael of Brea, which was built on the summit but pulled down in 1816 after it fell into decay.

It is said to have been inhabited by holy men or hermits, who were paid by the fishermen of St Just to keep a beacon burning to guide travellers and ships.

The summer solstice beacon fire on Chapel Carn Brea recalls the days when a holy man used to shine a light from this spot to warn passing ships.
NIGEL HOMER

One of these, Harry the Hermit, was said to be able to raise storms against fishermen who refused to pay his fees.

Indeed, in medieval times, it was a widespread standard practice for monks to provide lights on the coast to guide shipping. They took the form of a simple brazier or fire basket, and were known as ecclesiastical lights, often remembered only in cases of headlands taking on saints' names.

Truro's County Record Office has a manuscript recording the 'beaconage' received at Chapel Carn Brea (not to be confused with Carn Brea at Redruth) from the fisherman in 1396. This is the earliest record in Cornwall of lights being used as a navigational aid.

The practice is remembered today with an annual summer solstice bonfire lit on Chapel Carn Brea on 23 June. It is the first of an 80-mile chain of beacon fires lit across Cornwall, the next in the sequence being at Madron, and organised by the Old Cornwall Society since 1920.

CHAPTER TWENTY TWO
SEVEN STONES REEF

The current unmanned Seven Stones lightship, complete with solar panels. All the lightships are painted bright red to make them distinctive by day.
PETE MCPHAIL

ONCE UPON A TIME there was a beautiful kingdom lying to the west of Cornwall.

Said to have several towns and 140 churches, ruled by the City of Lyons, it was known as Lyonesse. However, it was engulfed by a tsunami and an earthquake and destroyed in a single night. Only the Scilly Isles and the rock around which the city was built, now known as the Seven Stones reef, survived.

The most popular legend has Merlin the wizard casting a spell to destroy Lyonesse and engulf the forces of the traitorous Mordred who were pursuing the forces of King Arthur, who he had just slain in battle. The tidal wave allowed Arthur's supporters to reach high ground in the form of the Scilly Isles.

Trinity House lightship No 80 which was stationed on the reef from 1914-58, and is now being restored in the River Medway. BEN HENDERSON

The legendary Trevelyan, who escaped the flood that destroyed Lyonesse on horseback, and the Padstow 'Obby 'Oss, thought by some to derive from that myth. GREAT WESTERN RAILWAY/ROBIN JONES

Another story tells how Lyonesse disappeared long after Arthur's time, deluged in the great storm of November 11 1099 which is well documented as destroying large parts of the English coast elsewhere.

Only one person survived, a man named Trevelyan who escaped the inrushing waves riding on a black horse and reached the safety of dry land. His escape is said to form the basis of Padstow's 'Obby 'Oss festivities on 1 May: indeed, as we saw at Trevose Head, the rocks lying out to sea line up directly with the mainland when viewed from a point near the lighthouse, highlighting the fact that the Cornish coast was once much further out than it is today.

How long ago, if at all within historical times, did this happen, is the key question, but Lyonesse has provided rich inspiration to poets, painters and dreamers for centuries, so why let the facts get in the way of a good story? As recently as the twentieth century, it was presented as fact that fishermen found fragments of doors and windows in their nets between Land's End and the Scillies, and that the roofs of houses could be seen in the depths below.

What is definitely true is that the Seven Stones reef, which lies ten miles off the coast of Land's End, has been a curse to shipping for centuries. Unlike other isolated rocks on which lighthouses have been built, it lies too far below low water for anyone to seriously consider building a traditional navigational beacon on it.

Something had to be done, however, and so in 1879, Trinity House moored the first of a long line of lightships there, in the most exposed position of any British light vessel.

The vessel originally had a crew of ten keepers, with five on station at a time. They probably had the fright of their lives 13 November 1872, when a meteor exploded above the ship and scattered cinders all over the deck.

An engineer carrying out lightship maintenance. TRINITY HOUSE

By the start of the twentieth century, most Trinity House lightships had a crew of 11, comprising a master and six ratings on board, and a master and three ratings ashore. The masters were changed every month, while the rest of the crew served a month afloat followed by two weeks of shore leave.

When a man started he would serve as a general seaman before being promoted to fog signal driver and lamplighter. After 15 to 20 years of service, he could graduate to the rank of master.

The most infamous wreck on the Seven Stones reef in modern times was that of the oil tanker *Torrey Canyon*, which came to grief on Pollard's Rock on 18 March 1967 due to a navigational error en route to Milford Haven.

During attempts to refloat the ship, Captain Stal of the Dutch salvage team was killed when he was blown overboard by an explosion.

Desperately trying in vain to prevent a major environmental disaster, Royal Navy vessels used detergent to try to disperse the oil, but the ship was already breaking up. What followed was the worst oil spill in British history.

The entire cargo of 860,000 barrels of oil was released into the Atlantic or burned during the next 12 days. The ship lost structural integrity on 26 March releasing further oil into the sea.

British Prime Minister Harold Wilson ordered the wreck to be bombed, to send as much oil as possible to the bottom with it. Blackburn Buccaneer planes from the Naval Air Station at Lossiemouth dropped 42 1,000lb bombs on the wreckage, with RAF Hawker Hunter jets adding cans of aviation fuel in the hope of burning the oil. However, exceptionally high tides extinguished the fire and a quarter of the bombs missed the 'sitting duck' target to the embarrassment of the RAF.

The thick black oil slick spread out over 270 square miles, with 120 miles of Cornish coastline and 50 miles of the French shores contaminated. All fish within a 75-mile radius and around 15,000 sea birds died.

The ship eventually sank and now lies at a depth of 98ft.

An inquiry in Liberia, where the ship was registered, blamed the captain, Pastrengo Rugiati, because he took a short cut to Milford Haven.

As with other lightships, a Trinity House supply ship was used to bring in new crew members to the Seven Stones vessel. However, in 1978, a helicopter landing pad was laid on the stern of the lightship.

Since 1987, the ship has been automated and unmanned. The accommodation and storage space was stripped out and filled with foam to ensure that she stays afloat in the event of a collision.

The lightship has broken free of her moorings on several occasions, and is now secured by a heavy chain to an anchor weighing more than four tons. In June 1999, she broke free from her moorings and began drifting towards Land's End – creating a hazard to passing ships which would have relied on her being in the exact location marked on their charts.

The ship emits three white flashes every 30 seconds and the fog signal issues three blasts every 60 seconds.

One of the Seven Stones lightships, Trinity House vessel No 80, has been preserved by husband and wife Ben and Gaelle Henderson, and is now moored in the River Medway in Kent.

She was built in 1914 of riveted iron and was specifically designed for the Seven Stones reef, the roughest station in Europe and accordingly was the biggest lightship to date at 116ft long.

In the winter of 1948 she broke her anchor chain and was adrift when rescued by Trinity House.

She served at Seven Stones until 1958, when she became a relief vessel to the east coast stations, and remained in service until 1975 when she was sold to the Ipswich Sea Cadets. The Hendersons bought her in 2006 and are slowly restoring her to her 1914 condition, despite the fact that all fittings had been removed.

The lamp of the former Seven Stones lightship No 80 now based in Kent.
BEN HENDERSON

CHAPTER TWENTY THREE
BISHOP ROCK

James Walker's first Bishop Rock lighthouse, washed away before it ever shone a light. ILLUSTRATED LONDON NEWS

THE FIRST AND LAST House at Land's End does not mark the frontier of civilisation. Neither do the Scilly Isles.

Four miles to the west of the Scillies, stands the bishop who would be king, beyond which, there certainly be dragons.

Bishop Rock lighthouse, which rears 167ft above the most ferocious of the Atlantic breakers, stands on what by a hair's breadth just about merits the classification of an island, albeit a miniscule one.

This brilliant piece of British engineering stands sentinel at the gateway to the country: Bishop Rock lighthouse, with its rooftop helipad. TRINITY HOUSE

This great circular granite sentinel marks the true start and end of Great Britain. It is the eastern end of the North Atlantic shipping route used by ocean liners in the first half of the twentieth century, the western end being the entrance to Lower New York Bay. The ship with the fastest time between these two points claimed the coveted Blue Riband.

It is often described as the King of all lighthouses, although it is the second highest in Britain, behind Eddystone, because it boasts one of the finest feats of lighthouse engineering to be found around any shores.

It was built to warn ships off the multitude of jagged pinnacles that make up the Western Rocks, which had regularly claimed the lives of sailors since shipping began.

The most notorious wreck of all was that of Admiral of the Fleet Sir Cloudesley Shovell's flagship HMS *Association* on 22 October 1707, along with HMS *Eagle*, HMS *Romney* and HMS *Firebrand* returning from Gibraltar to Portsmouth after taking part in an unsuccessful attempt to seize the French port of Toulon during the War of the Spanish Succession. Between 1,400 and 2,000 sailors depending on reports were drowned in what became known as the Scilly Naval Disaster.

In bad weather, Shovell believed that they were sailing past the French island of Ushant,

James Walker, engineer in chief at Trinity House.

An eighteenth-century engraving of the great Scilly Naval Disaster of 1707.

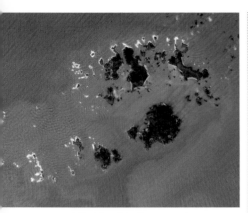

The Isles of Scilly as seen from space. Bishop Rock is in the far south-western corner, on the edge of the Western Rocks. NASA

The lighthouse as seen from sea level today. RICHARD KNIGHTS*

but were way off course and heading straight for the Scillies.

Shovell's 90-gun ship crashed into the Outer Gilstone Rock and sank within four minutes, taking him with it. His body was washed up seven miles away in Porthellick Cove on St Mary's the next day, and he was eventually buried in Westminster Abbey. The wreckage of HMS *Association* on the Gilstone Ledge was not discovered until 1967.

The disaster led to the Longitude Act in 1714, which established the Board of Longitude and offered a substantial money prize to anyone who could devise a method of accurately determining longitude. The prize led to the development of accurate marine chronometers, and the lunar distance method, by which the angle between the moon and another celestial body is used to calculate position, was developed.

It was also eventually decided that the navigational warning system for the Scilly Isles, which at the time consisted only of the coal-fired lighthouse on St Agnes, was utterly inadequate.

So James Walker, engineer-in-chief at Trinity House, built a new type of lighthouse to be on the archipelago's westernmost extremity, the hard pink granite islet known as Bishop Rock.

He argued that building a traditional stone tower on Bishop Rock would be impossible because the ledge was too small, and it would not withstand the tremendous seas and gales, with wind pressures occasionally exceeding 7,000 lb per square foot.

His design was a 138ft tall screw-pile skeletal lighthouse erected on cast iron legs supported by wrought iron rods, so that the huge waves would crash through the piles instead of buffeting a stone tower.

Trinity House gave the go-ahead for the £12,000 lighthouse in 1847 and it was completed within two years. However, a light was never shown, because it collapsed in a gale on 5 February 1850 before one could fitted, and the sea quickly carried away the wreckage.

Walker withdrew his opposition to a stone tower and devised a fresh scheme based on Smeaton's third Eddystone lighthouse. Walker's Tower was built with a 33ft diameter on a rock ledge just 151ft long by 52ft wide, rising sheer from the seabed 148ft below.

Because Bishop Rock is so isolated, even from the rest of the Scillies, workmen were based in stone cottages and workshops erected on the tiny uninhabited isle of Rosevean, which became the site of Britain's most south-westerly houses, the ruins of which can still be seen.

Stonemasons on Rosevean received supplies of uncut granite from the quarries at Lamorna and Carnsew on the mainland and cut and shaped it, before numbering each finished block. The blocks were then transported to Bishop Rock, where the 115ft tower slowly took shape, each block weighing between one and two tons.

Each course of masonry was dovetailed and keyed into position at the sides, top and the bottom, to effectively provide a bastion of solid, immovable rock.

Even at the lowest tides, the rock ledge lay more than a foot under the sea. A coffer dam was built and the water was pumped out to leave a dry area for the masons to lay the foundation blocks 10ft below low water.

A total of 25,000 tons of stone were used to build it. It took seven years to complete, cost £34,560 and was described square foot by square foot as Britain's most expensive building site of all time.

Using a wick lamp, the first light was shone by the keepers on 1 September 1858. A triumph of British engineering, it was rightly hailed as a masterpiece around the world. Bishop Rock therefore became what was recognised a century later as the world's smallest inhabited island.

The ability of the lighthouse to stand up to the worst Atlantic weather that could be thrown at it amazed all, although it was said to vibrate, on at least one occasion causing some of the glass in the lantern to shatter, and during one storm, waves rode up on one the side of the tower and ripped away the 550lb fog bell from its fastenings in the gallery. The tower had to be strengthened with iron rods.

Sir James Douglass inspected the lighthouse in 1881 and discovered widespread damage and weakness in the tower caused by the pounding wave action.

Trinity House agreed to strengthen the tower and to increase its height by 39ft. A massive cylindrical granite base was designed as added protection against the force of the waves, reducing their strength before they hit the tower itself. Massive blocks of granite were sunk into the rock and fastened by heavy bolts, providing a masonry casing more than 3ft thick,

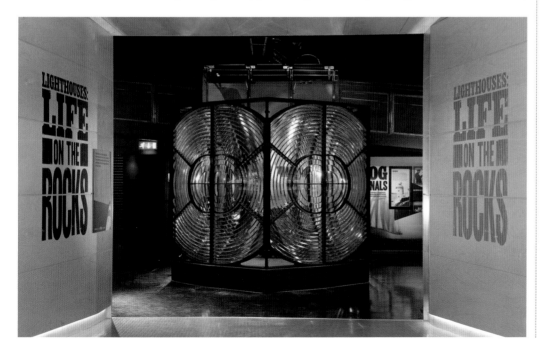

One half of the giant Bishop Rock double Fresnel lens can be seen in the National Maritime Museum Cornwall at Falmouth. The other half is still in use on the lighthouse. NMMC

In 1969, the same year as man first walked on the moon, this was the time-honoured means by which lighthouse keepers still used to access Bishop Rock, a striking image displayed in the National Maritime Museum Cornwall's lighthouse exhibition.
GIBSONS OF SCILLY/COURTESY NMMC

A Trinity House helicopter taking off from St Just airfield.
TRINITY HOUSE

extending upwards to the point where the new stonework for the extended height of the light began. By building a new casing around Walker's original lighthouse, Douglass was in effect constructing a second one.

The £66,000 improvements were finished in October 1887, and Bishop Rock lighthouse has stood firm ever since.

Changing keeper shifts and landing supplies, however, was always a precarious business. A rope was swung between the supply vessel and the base of the lighthouse and the keepers were winched along it using a type of harness to reach one or the other.

In 1936, for the only time in history, a bishop visited Bishop Rock – and used the same rope method as the keepers to be hauled 'aboard'. In full Church of England dress, the Bishop of Truro, Cornishman Joseph Hunkin, was lifted 30ft into the air, accompanied by his chaplain, E.C. Seager, to perform a confirmation ceremony for the two keepers on duty.

Many visitors were lashed to the rope for safety when they were taken up. The lighthouse was the last to use a hand winch.

The access problem was finally sorted in 1976 when a helipad was built on the top of the lantern, and from then on the lighthouse was reached only by helicopter from St Just airfield near Land's End.

The lighthouse, which has a focal plane of 144ft, was electrified in 1973, replacing the oil vapour lamp and mantle with a 400-watt electric version.

The lighthouse has ten floors. In recent times, the base contained the water storage tanks set in the floor, with the main fuel oil stored on the floor above, along with the electric fuel distribution pump.

The next floor up comprised the lower engine room and workshop, with two generators. On the floor above were three oil tanks which gravity fed to the engine room below, and a gas-powered shower.

Next up was the kitchen, with a table in the middle and fixed benches on one side, and a gas cooker. This floor was said to be so cramped that diners ran the risk of striking their heads on the cooker's projecting extractor hood.

The floor above contained the bedroom with curved bunks and an electric storage heater. The next floor up contained the sitting room, which originally had a fireplace and the weight tube – dropping a weight down it turned the lantern optic – which was removed when the lighthouse was electrified. It also had three radio transmitters and the lighthouse's television set.

Further up the stairs, the next floor contained the service room, with two small engines to provide daylight power and a pair of compressed air engines for the fog signal. Finally, above this was the floor containing the lighthouse's very unusual 'double' Fresnel lens, a whopping 12ft high and 10ft in diameter, installed during the Douglass improvements.

It consisted of two giant lenses, each illuminated by a separate wick burner at first, but only the lower one was used in the main. Both lights, however, were lit in the fog.

Half of this unusual lens remains in use on Bishop Rock, while the other half, the top set, is on display at the National Maritime Museum Cornwall in Falmouth, which ran a special exhibition on lighthouses from 2010-11 and contains many key lighthouse exhibits.

The top floor also contained a toilet bucket, which was used and then emptied out into the passing wind.

The loneliest job in Britain finally came to an end on 21 December 1992 when the unpainted grey lighthouse became fully automated after being converted the year before. The only visitors are Trinity House service engineers who access the light from the roof.

Today's rotating light, which has an intensity of 600,000 candela, emits two white flashes every 15 seconds and has a range of 24 nautical miles. The fog signal was discontinued on 13 June 2007.

Isolated it may be, but millions of TV viewers see Bishop Rock lighthouse every night, with a clip of a helicopter hovering directly above the helipad preceding many BBC news programmes.

The monotony broken: two keepers come out to see a boat load of tourists passing Bishop Rock. DAVID LALLY*

CHAPTER TWENTY FOUR
ST AGNES

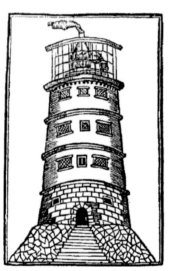

A drawing of St Agnes lighthouse from 1690.

ALONG WITH ITS LITTLE sister Gugh to which it is linked by a low-tide sandbar, St Agnes is the fourth biggest of the Scilly islands and covers just over half a square mile and has around 70 residents.

Landmarks include the Old Man of Gugh, a standing stone, the Troy Town Maze, believed to date from medieval times, the Turk's Head pub, a post office and general store. However, the real trademark of St Agnes is its lighthouse. Indeed, at one stage, St Agnes was also known as the Lighthouse Island.

Built in 1680 by Trinity House, it is the second oldest in Cornwall, and one of the oldest in Britain. Its 70ft somewhat bulbous white-painted round stone tower, is located on the highest point of the island, 138ft above mean high water.

It was constructed by Captains Hugh Till and Symon Bayly, builders of the 1676 Lowestoft lighthouse, in three stages, with a pair of adjoining two-storey keepers' houses, also painted white.

The lamp was provided originally by a coal fire without a lens, burning in a large open basket called a chauffer, now preserved and on display in Tresco Abbey Gardens. It was said that its primitive light could be seen more than 20 miles away.

A visitor in 1750 recorded that the keeper was paid £40 a year, with his assistant getting £20, and they were well worth the money, as their predecessor had often let the fire go out.

High-quality smokeless coal was supplied by ship once a year and a carriage hired to carry it to the lighthouse, at "an agreeable benefit to the poor inhabitants". Until the islands were revolutionised by the flower industry in the nineteenth century following the coming of the railway to Penzance, and their discovery by tourists and yachtsmen, the Scillies were one of the poorest regions of Britain, where the inhabitants eked out a meagre existence, often relying on shellfish.

It was said that more ships were wrecked on St Agnes, because of its position to the Western Rocks, than on any other part of the Scilly archipelago. Far from regretting this fact, the often-hungry inhabitants thanked the local saint St Warna, who they believed sent the ships to their doom so that the islanders could benefit from the wreckage. St Agnes folk celebrated the saint with a feast day once a year following "certain superstitious ceremonies."

Around 1780, the coal fire was replaced by an oil lamp on a circular wick. That provoked

St Agnes lighthouse stands on the highest point of the island.
STAN ANDREW

complaints that the light had diminished, and could not be distinguished from that of a passing ship, or even seen at all. On 4 September 1783, the *Financier*, bound for London with tobacco, rice and indigo from Carolina, was smashed to pieces on nearby rocks within 15 minutes, with the loss of three lives. In the same hour, the *Nancy*, carrying rum and sugar from Jamaica, was wrecked a mile from the lighthouse, but everyone aboard was saved. A third ship was also believed to have been lost with all hands at the same time.

An image of tranquillity: St Agnes lighthouse overlooks the island pond. TIM DOBSON*

Improvements were made in 1790 with the fitting of the rotary light mechanism by inventor Adam Walker, a travelling science lecturer whose syllabus included astronomy, engineering and optics. The new oil-fired light had copper lamps and 21 revolving reflectors.

In 1911, the St Agnes lighthouse was superseded by a far more basic structure on the island.

Peninnis lighthouse comprises a simple metal framework tower 46ft in height, the upper part painted white with the lower part and cupola painted black. Originally lit by acetylene gas, it was converted to electricity when it was fully automated in 1992.

Standing 118ft above mean high water, the rotating optic lens emits a white flash every 20 seconds and, with an intensity of 4,500 candela, it has a range of 17 nautical miles, but it was planned to reduce its range under the Trinity House 2010 Aids to Navigation review. The original St Agnes lighthouse now serves only as a white-painted daymark. The lighthouse is a private dwelling although outbuildings within the complex are available as holiday accommodation through St Agnes Lighthouse Farm Holiday Lets.

Nearly as old as the original lighthouse is a daymark built at the north-east corner of the island of St Martins in 1683, not 1637 as a date on the blocked entrance arch incorrectly states. The 36ft tall somewhat stumpy rendered granite circular tower, which is 16ft in diameter below the cone, was the work of Thomas Ekins, the first steward of the landowner Godophin family to live on the Scillies.

The earliest surviving dated example of a beacon in Britain, it was painted white until 1822. By 1833 it had been painted red, and now carries bands of red and white.

CHAPTER TWENTY FIVE
ROUND ISLAND

These cottages overlooking Porth Cressa at the Scilly capital of Hugh Town, St Agnes, were Trinity House homes for the keepers of Bishop Rock and Round Island lighthouses until both were automated.
DAVID LALLY*

THE BUILDING OF A lighthouse on Round Island, the most northerly outpost of the Scillies, was a massive feat not only of engineering but of endurance.

Contractors had to lift the building materials to the 115ft top of the plateau-like island, where the sheer cliff face made the job almost impossible and hardly bearable.

A set of keepers' cottages was built, adding Round Island to the elite list of Scilly Isles inhabited in the past century, alongside St Mary's, St Martin's, Tresco, Bryher and St Agnes and Gugh.

However, people lived on it in prehistoric times, when it may have formed part of a large land mass. Indeed, a cairn or burial chamber was destroyed to make way for the 62ft tall granite ashlar lighthouse tower, designed by William Tregarthen Douglass, chief engineer for the Commissioners of Irish Lights in the late nineteenth and early twentieth centuries and a consulting engineer for lighthouse construction for several governments around the world.

An aerial view of the lighthouse complex. TRINITY HOUSE

Coming from a famous family of lighthouse engineers, his father was the previously-mentioned Sir James Nicholas Douglass. His uncle William and his grandfather Nicholas were also leading figures in lighthouse construction.

The only access by foot to the Round Island lighthouse was up a flight of steps hewn out of the solid rock. Supplies were taken up the rock face by an aerial hoist.

The light, which has a focal plane of 180ft, was first shone in 1887, and with St Agnes and the Bishop, completed a ring of navigation aids around a group of small islands with treacherous rocks.

An enormous hyperradial optic, 15ft high and weighing more than eight tons, was fitted to the Round Island light. This type was installed at only two other lighthouses at the beginning of the twentieth century.

It was replaced in 1966 with more modern apparatus that lasted until the lighthouse was automated in 1987, leaving the little island deserted once more.

The 360mm revolving optic emits one white flash every 10 seconds. It has an intensity of 340,000 candela and a range of 24 nautical miles. The fog signal emits four blasts every 60 seconds.

The lighthouse, now accessed only by helicopter, is a Grade 2 listed building.

CHAPTER TWENTY SIX
WOLF ROCK

SAILORS HAVE GOOD REASON to fear the howl of the Wolf.

Four nautical miles south west of Land's End lies a single rock, where its fissures emit a weird howling sound when filled by the Atlantic winds. Accordingly, it was named Wolf Rock.

Lieutenant Henry Smith obtained power to build a navigational mark on Wolf Rock from Trinity House in 1791. So instead of a stone tower, he settled for a 20ft high wrought iron mast daymark – with no light – four inches in diameter, supported by six stays. On top of the mast was placed a metal effigy of a wolf.

Four years later, it was washed out to sea.

John Thurburn built a beacon on the rock in the late 1830s. It was finished in the middle of 1840, but by November that year, it too had been swept away.

Wolf Rock lighthouse seen from the air.
TRINITY HOUSE

Next it was the turn of Trinity House builder James Walker, who constructed a 14ft high cone-shaped iron beacon on Wolf Rock, using iron plates filled with cement rubble. Conditions in the Atlantic were so bad that the construction team managed just 302 hours in five years. Unlike its predecessors, Walker's beacon survived, and today forms part of the landing stage.

Trinity House knew that a better light was needed, and so in July 1861, engineer James Douglass surveyed Wolf Rock and began building one the following March.

Again, it was a case of battling against the full force of nature. Because of the conditions, the builders managed to land only 22 times in 1862, and then they often had to battle their way through the raging waves to get on and off the rock. By 1864, they were still struggling to complete the second course of masonry.

Walker designed the granite tower, again basing it on Smeaton's third Eddystone lighthouse. One special feature at Wolf Rock was the ingenious and highly effective design of the dovetailed joints on the lower masonry courses, intended to prevent the water erosion of the cement. The upper surface of each stone, which were cut to size and shaped in Penzance, was sculpted with a wide rebate and the stone above fitted into the recess in order that that the horizontal joint between the two was covered by the outer fillet, giving total protection, up to a height of 39ft.

A total of 3,297 tons of stone was used to build the tower, which cost £62,276 and stands

Wolf Rock on a calm day: the cone on the right-hand side is James Walker's 1840 daymark. ALVARO*

An early twentieth-century hand-coloured view of the lighthouse minus, of course, the modern helipad. ROBIN JONES COLLECTION

at 135ft with a focal plane of 112ft, and a base diameter of nearly 42ft tapering to 17ft. The walls are 8ft thick in places, while the entrance door was cast from gun metal in two halves, together weighing a ton, to withstand the force of the sea.

Another 1,078 tons were required to build the landing platform which, once completed, allowed a crane for loading and unloading the stone blocks to be installed and make the building work far more effective and efficient in what were still appalling conditions.

Finally, the lighthouse was finished on 19 July 1869, and the light was shone, using an oil lamp, in January 1870.

To access the rock from landing boats, the keepers who lived inside the tower while on duty were swung ashore by the crane.

Wolf Rock was one of the first lighthouses to use Arthur Kitson's pressurised vapour burner lamp, which appeared in 1901.

The lighthouse was converted to electricity in 1955, when a generator was installed.

An 1870 diagram of the lighthouse and its interior. INSTITUTE OF CIVIL ENGINEERS

In 1972, it became the first lighthouse in the world to be fitted with a helipad, which subsequently became a standard feature on many lighthouses.

In July 1988, the last keepers were withdrawn when it became automatic. Today, the only access for service engineers is by helicopter and entering through the roof of the lantern.

The 1,500-watt lamp has an intensity of 378,000 candela and emits a white flash every 15 seconds, with a range of 23 nautical miles. The fog signal sounds a five-second blast once every 30 seconds. The unpainted grey stone lighthouse with its white lantern can be distantly seen from Land's End during the day as well as at night.

Despite what navigational aids are provided here, whether they take the form of a traditional lighthouse or high-tech equipment, never forget: this Wolf is forever hungry.

Signpost at Land's End. STUART PRESTON*

CHAPTER TWENTY SEVEN
LONGSHIPS

THE ROMANS HAD A name for Land's End – Belerion, the 'seat of the storm'.

Constantly buffeted by the Atlantic wind and waves, the westernmost part of the British mainland is surrounded by jagged rocks and sheer cliffs. For the painter, artist or daytripper, they are romantic. For the sailor, they are merciless.

Around one-and-a-quarter miles to the west of Land's End is a group of rocks which are named after their resemblance to the shape of maritime vessels of times past – Longships.

These rocks are submerged at high water, apart from the three biggest - Carn Bras, Tal-y-Maen and Meinek, are covered only by storm waves and spray. Between the Longships and the coast are two smaller rocks called Kettle's Bottom.

Carn Bras is the highest point of the Longships, rising to 39ft above sea level.

It was on this rock that the first Longships lighthouse was built.

Until the last decade of the eighteenth century, Land's End was feared by seamen but a friend to landlubbers. When a ship was dashed to pieces on the rocks, poverty-stricken locals would see the wreckage as a windfall. Grounded ships would be plundered for everything that could be carried away, from the cargo down to the timbers, and each winter, there would be shipwrecks aplenty.

Trinity House obtained a patent to build a lighthouse on 30 June 1791, and awarded a lease to Lieutenant Henry Smith to do so.

The circular tower was designed by Trinity House architect Samuel Wyatt, It had three storeys; the lowest containing water tanks and stores, the next comprising a living room and the top one, with the keepers sleeping beneath the wood and copper lantern, which towered 79ft over the waves, and cooking their meals on the jets that served the lantern.

The lantern held 18 parabolic metal reflectors and Argand lamps, set in two tiers. The fixed light was shone for the first time on 29 September 1795.

However, the jubilant Smith was soon afterwards declared "incapable of managing his affairs" and ended up in a debtors' prison. The Court of Chancery took over his business interests and paid what profits there were to his family.

The lighthouse was staffed by four men, with two on duty at any one time, and shifts lasting a month. They were paid £30 a year and their food while on duty was free, but when they were back on shore, they had to seek alternative employment.

An aerial view of Longships lighthouse today. TRINITY HOUSE

A storm breaking over Longships lighthouse. TIM STEVENS/COURTESY NATIONAL MARITIME MUSEUM CORNWALL

It was claimed, though not verified, that one 'raw' keeper was driven insane by his experience amidst the howling gales and crashing waves. Indeed, because of the height of the waves during storms, the lantern was so often obscured by water that it was useless at the very time it was needed the most.

Trinity House eventually bought out the lease with just under a decade remaining, and in 1869, engineer Sir James Douglass began replacing the original tower with a new one

One of the glorious sunsets for which Land's End is famous, with the arch known as Enys Dodman in the foreground and the lighthouse near the horizon to the left. JIM CHAMPION*

Longships lighthouse framed by the cavern beneath Land's End, in a 1907 view. ROBIN JONES COLLECTION

alongside built out of grey granite, with a focal plane of 115ft.

The construction used much of the equipment from the building of the Wolf Rock lighthouse. The first light, this time using a pressure vapour lamp with an incandescent mantle, was shone in December 1873, the intensity having been increased to 72,000 candela and the range to 17½ miles. After the tower was completed, the original lighthouse was demolished: in 1874, the rock on which it had stood split.

Yet the Longships still remained a great danger to shipping. On 10 November 1898, the steamship *Bluejacket* ran aground on the rocks on a clear night and nearly wrecked the lighthouse too. However, the crew had a luckier escape than most as all 22 were rescued by the Sennen lifeboat.

When on shore, the keepers lived with their families in tied cottages at Mayon, above Sennen Cove. It was said that the keepers used to communicate with their wives by using semaphore and telescopes. Incidentally, the Longships are mostly in Sennen parish, and may therefore be civically, if not physically, the westernmost point of the mainland.

It was in 1966 that the lighthouse became one of the first to have supplies sent out by helicopter, despite the difficulty in landing.

In 1967, the lighthouse was electrified, and in 1974, a helipad was built on the top.

Longships became automated in 1988.

The white light, which has an intensity of 40,500 candela comprises one five-second flash every ten seconds when seen from seaward, but shows red sectors if a ship gets too near to Gwennap Head or Cape Cornwall, which was long erroneously thought to be the British mainland's westernmost point before measurements correctly identified it as Land's End. The light has a range of 18 nautical miles. The fog signal sounds a one-second blast every ten seconds.

Despite the massive improvements in ship navigation, with high tech and satellite equipment, the rocks around Land's End will never cease to claim vessels that get it wrong, without a second thought.

CHAPTER TWENTY EIGHT

TATER DU AND THE RUNNELSTONE

IT WAS EARLY ON 23 October 1963 that during a south-westerly gale in conditions of poor visibility, Spanish coaster the *Juan Ferrer* ran aground at Boscawen Point on the south coast of Penwith, about a mile-and-a-half west of Lamorna Cove. Part of the cargo included shotguns made in Spain.

The crew sent a Mayday call before the engine room filled with water and all power was lost.

One of the lifeboats was launched, only to be dashed against the rocks before it drifted back out to sea. Some of the crew managed to jump on to the rocks and escaped, but 11 died. The captain was saved by a clifftop rescue team as he clung to pieces of floating wreckage.

The tragedy led to calls by the Newlyn and Mousehole Fisherman's Association to build a new lighthouse, which Trinity House duly did. Designed by Michael H. Crisp, and built by Humphreys of Knightsbridge, it was completed in July 1965.

It is the newest of all of the Cornish lighthouses, and unlike the others, was automatic and unmanned from the start. The tower was built from white concrete blocks, with a 7ft 1in lantern on top, and a focal plane of 112ft.

The 49ft tall lighthouse is accessed down a steep path, with a sign warning users that the foghorn at a point halfway along can be heard at 100 decibels.

The steep path down to Tater Du lighthouse. TONY ATKIN

Tater Du lighthouse on a calm day in the waters around Penwith.
ROGER HOLLINGSWORTH

Cornwall's newest lighthouse – the honeycombed front of Tater Du.
MITCH REES

The electric light is operated by batteries charged continually from the mains, and will run for five days should the supply fail, in which case a backup generator is at hand.

The main light has three white flashes every 15 seconds, and fixed 111ft above mean sea level, has a range of 23 nautical miles.

There is a separate red fixed sector light that shows in the line over the Runnel Stone, or Runnelstone Rock, with a range of 13 nautical miles, at an intensity of 294,000 candela. There is a separate fixed red sector light with an intensity of 11,100 candela, with a range of 13 nautical miles, and shows in the line over the Runnel Stone rock nearly five miles to the west.

The fog signal was originally a series of 72 speaker units built into the honeycombed front of the lighthouse tower, which was designed to hold an array of sound signals. This system was superseded by a short-range Pharos Marine Omnidirectional electric emitter sounding the same two one-second blasts every 30 seconds during fog.

The lighthouse, which oversees the Inner and Outer Bucks, two rocks that partially appear at low tide, where the SS *Garonne* sank in 1868, was modernised during 1996/7.

The Runnel Stone presents a major hazard to shipping a mile south of Gwennap Head. Indeed, between 1880 and 1923, more than 30 steamships came to grief in the locality. The stone's pinnacle could be seen above the surface until it was hit by a steamship in 1923.

A cardinal marker buoy now marks its position, equipped with a flashing light, a bell which sounds as the waves move, and a whistle set in a tube, which emits an eerie moaning tone which can be heard on the mainland.

Gwennap Head has a pair of cone-shaped day markers which also line up with the Runnel Stone buoy. The cone on the seaward side is painted red while its inland counterpart is black and white, and was placed in position by Trinity House in 1821. Ships must always keep the black and white one in sight so as to avoid the submerged rocks nearer the shore. If the black and white cone is completely obscured by the red cone, then the ship is directly over the Runnel Stone.

Far right: The Runnel Stone marker buoy.

Right: The Gwennap Head day marker cones which protect ships from the Runnel Stone. JIM CHAMPION*

CHAPTER TWENTY NINE

NEWLYN HARBOUR

FISHING HAS BEEN THE livelihood of Newlyn since time immemorial: indeed, the name is thought to originate from the Cornish for "pool for a fleet of boats". The natural protection provided by the Gwavas Lake area of Mounts Bay helped make it into a major fishing port, indeed the biggest in the locality.

Like St Ives, Newlyn became a magnet for artists from Victorian times onwards, and also has a harbour lighthouse, at the end of its South Pier. The white-painted 34ft tall round cast iron tower with red lantern was erected in 1914.

Of greater global significance is the little red-and-white painted building which stands next to the lighthouse. It was in here that in 1915, the Ordnance Survey established its tidal observatory, from which all heights in Britain were calculated.

Newlyn South Pier lighthouse, with the Ordnance Survey tidal observatory next to it, and St Michael's Mount on the other side of Mount's Bay in the background. ROGER HOLLINGSWORTH

An extract from the Ordnance Survey One-Inch Provisional Series map of 1946 shows the pier lighthouse and its next-door neighbour the tidal observatory, the point from where all the contours and heights on every one of its maps are derived.
ORDNANCE SURVEY

Right: *An Ordnance Survey metal flush bracket benchmark in Baston, Lincolnshire: this and hundreds of thousands of other benchmarks record heights based on Newlyn.*
ROBIN JONES

Far right: *An Ordnance Survey benchmark at Ancaster in Lincolnshire, one of tens of thousands throughout Britain based on measurements taken next to Newlyn's harbour lighthouse.*
ROBIN JONES

From 1 May 1915 to 30 April 1921, the Ordnance Survey used an automatic tide gauge to compile measurements of tidal height every 15 minutes. The average measurements were used to compile mean sea level, known as Ordnance Datum Newlyn, a common horizontal plane on which all mapped contour lines and spot heights were based.

Starting at Newlyn and working outwards across every part of the UK mainland, a complete survey on the country based on the Datum was carried out manually using land levelling equipment.

Accordingly, the UK Fundamental Benchmark was established here, and is set in the floor of the observatory. It stands 15.583ft above the Datum. A plaque mounted on the outside wall of the observatory commemorated the bicentenary of the Ordnance Survey in 1991.

The lighthouse, which often takes a pounding in rough seas, has a focal plane of 34ft and emits a white flash every five seconds which is visible for nine to ten miles. A foghorn gives one blast every 60 seconds. It is operated by the Newlyn Pier and Harbour Commission.

CHAPTER THIRTY
PENZANCE HARBOUR

PENZANCE, THE MAINLAND port for the Isles of Scilly, takes its name from the Cornish word for 'holy headland', because the chapel of St Anthony stood for more than a millennium to the west of today's harbour. It was first mentioned as a fishing port in 1322.

Penzance began to take off after Henry IV granted it a market charter. Another boost came when Henry VIII awarded the right to charge harbour dues, while James I elevated it to borough status.

A calm day on the lighthouse pier.
TED DALE

The first harbour pier was built in 1512, with the southern arm, which dates from 1766, extended in 1785 and 1812. The first harbour lighthouse was built on it in 1817.

In 1814, John Matthews opened the first dry dock in the town there.

The problem of land communication with the rest of Britain began to be solved big time with the opening of the West Cornwall railway to Redruth on 11 March 1852, the station being on the eastern side of the harbour. With the opening of Brunel's Royal Saltash Bridge on 4 May 1859, Penzance was linked to Bristol and London, opening up markets local fishermen could have only dreamed about before.

The railway spurred bigger improvements to the harbour, with the Albert Pier being built on the eastern side of the harbour in 1853, when a new harbour lighthouse replaced the earlier one when the south pier was extended.

Standing at the end of the pier, its 31ft round cylindrical cast iron tower was prefabricated by the Copperhouse Foundry at Hayle.

With a focal plane of 37ft, it emits a flash every five seconds, white to the south east and red in other directions. The pier also became known as the Lighthouse Pier.

The lighthouse, managed by Penzance Harbour Users Association, stands near the Isles of Scilly ferry terminal.

Because of its dry dock and engineering facilities, Trinity House chose Penzance as its western depot, which opened in 1866 and serviced all the lighthouses and lightships between Trevose Head and Start Point. The depot's Buoy Store was later turned into the Trinity House National Lighthouse Museum, which closed in 2005 with its exhibits dispersed to other heritage venues, including the National Maritime Museum Cornwall in Falmouth.

The Scillonian III *berthed alongside the Penzance harbour lighthouse.*
ISLES OF SCILLY TOURISM

An 1840s engraving entitled Penzance and Stone Pier, showing the old pier dating from 1766 on the right, with the original lighthouse.

CHAPTER THIRTY ONE
MARAZION AND ST MICHAEL'S MOUNT

THIS SMALL WHITEWASHED octagonal single storey crenelated building in the grounds of a former vicarage at Marazion in Mount's Bay is said to have acted as a lighthouse for its former harbour at some stage, although historical evidence for this is at best scant.

Grade 2 listed, and said to date from the mid to late nineteenth century, English Heritage describes the building as a gazebo. It was said that a fashion for castles and Gothic structures seems to have affected Marazion in the nineteenth century, maybe inspired by the island of St Michael's Mount and its fairytale castle which stand on the far side of a tidal causeway from Marazion.

English Heritage said that the gazebo is the most modern of these fanciful structures, sited prominently opposite the Mount.

Marazion is Cornwall's oldest chartered town, receiving its charter in 1257. At the time it was more important than Penzance, two miles further west. Many people believe its name comes from 'Market Jew', but it originates from Marghas Byhgan, Cornish for 'little market.'

The church on St Michael's Mount has the remains of a stone lantern which is believed to have been installed in the fifteenth century as a navigational aid for the island harbour.

The Marazion 'gazebo' from which a guiding light may have been shown long ago. IAN WRIGHT

Marazion and its position to St Michael's Mount, which may have had a beacon on the top of its church in the fifteenth century. The gazebo 'lighthouse' is on the far edge of the mainland shore. SHIROKAZAN*

CHAPTER THIRTY TWO
LIZARD POINT

LIZARD POINT IS THE MOST southerly part of the British mainland, and the point where most ships first sight land as they enter the English Channel. Because of the rocks that lie in the waters off the headland, it is also one of the most dangerous, and presents a major obstacle to the natural deepwater port of Falmouth.

The site of countless maritime disasters, the seaways round the Lizard peninsula were known as the 'graveyard of ships'.

To the east lie the Manacles, one-and-a-half square miles of razor-sharp rocks lurking just beneath the surface.

The name Lizard probably derives from the Cornish 'Lys Ardh' meaning 'high court' and has nothing to do with reptiles, although much of it is comprised by the highly-prized metamorphic rock known as serpentine.

The lighthouse complex showing both towers and the foghorn at the far left.
TRINITY HOUSE

It was in 1619 that what is regarded as Cornwall's oldest light was established by Cornishman Sir John Killigrew on Lizard Point, to anger both near and far. The locals were fearful that there would be a sharp fall in the number of wrecks, and therefore less free pickings from the shoreline. Also, Trinity House disliked the idea of someone else having control over a lighthouse, even though it was not prepared to build one itself.

Killigrew went ahead, after agreeing to a condition to turn the light off should enemy vessels and pirates approach, in case it guided them to a safe landing. He agreed to pay a rent of "20 nobles a year" (33p) for 30 years hoping to charge fees from ship-owners towards its upkeep.

Fury erupted again when, against the advice of Trinity House, James I tried to extract fees from passing ships himself. When ship owners opposed the tax, the patent to operate the light was withdrawn and the tower demolished in 1630.

Lizard lighthouse and staff pictured in 1908. TRINITY HOUSE

The wreck of the 44-gun frigate HMS *Anson* at Loe Bar in 1807 in which over 100 seamen drowned, inspired inventor Henry Trengrouse to devise the 'Rocket' life-saving apparatus after failing to come up with an adequate lifeboat. His invention later became the Breeches buoy, a device used to swing a rope either from ship to ship, or ship to shore, using a rocket gun.

The idea of a lighthouse at Lizard Point was resurrected in 1751 by Thomas Fonnereau, a London merchant and MP for Sudbury and Aldeburgh and a member of the Free British Fishery Society. The following year, Trinity House awarded him a lease on twin octagonal stone towers that he built at the point, for 61 years at an annual rent of £80.

The Lizard lighthouse optic. CHRIS ALLEN*

A turned serpentine lighthouse produced at Lizard Town. JOHN HILL/ CORNISH SERPENTINE WORKS

Inside the Lizard Lighthouse Heritage Centre. TRINITY HOUSE

Each of the lights was lit by a coal fire, and an 'overlooker' lived in a cottage between them, checking to see that each keeper maintained a sufficiently-bright light. The overlooker lay on a couch, with a window on either side through which he could see the lanterns. When the bellows blowers slackened and the fires diminished, he would 'wake' them up with a blast on a cowhorn.

Fonnerau's Lizard lighthouse looks much the same today.

Trinity House took over responsibility for the lighthouse in 1771. Argand oil lamps with reflectors were introduced in 1812, and in 1878, a foghorn was added.

Fresh from his activities on Flat Holm, Marconi's famous transatlantic wireless experiments took place on the Lizard in December 1901, when he sent a radio communication to St John's, Newfoundland, from his transmitter station on the cliffs above Poldhu. Before that, he stayed at the Housel Bay Hotel near Lizard Point and leased a plot in an adjoining wheat field to erect his Lizard Wireless Telegraph Station, a wooden hut, near the signal station which had been built by Lloyd's of London to report ship arrivals. In January 1901, Marconi received what was then the distance record signal, 186 miles, from his transmitter at Niton on the Isle of Wight.

A selection of marine buoys along the entrance path leading to the heritage centre. TRINITY HOUSE

The Lizard Wireless Station, which was restored by the National Trust, is the oldest Marconi station to survive in its original state anywhere in the world.

In 1903, the lighthouse's two fixed lights were changed, and the one in the western tower was switched off altogether. The eastern tower continued in use, with a single flashing light from an arc lamp.

The lighthouse was fully electrified in 1924.

The 62ft tall east tower, which has a focal plane of 230ft, emits a white flash every three seconds from its rotating optic, with an intensity of 800,000 candela and a range of 26 nautical miles. The foghorn sounds every 30 seconds.

In 1998 the lighthouse was automated, and later the six keepers' cottages became holiday lets.

On 13 July 2009, Princess Anne opened Trinity House's Lizard Lighthouse Heritage Centre in the engine room, which still features some of the original engines.

A series of interactive exhibits and displays focus on the history of the lighthouse, the life of a keeper, and the part that lighthouses play in sea safety.

Visitors can power up and sound a foghorn, track ships, send a message using Morse code, learn about semaphore and signal flags, climb the lighthouse tower and hear keepers' stories and learn about living in and working on a lighthouse.

You can even take your own working electric lighthouse home from the Scilly Isles. Lizard Town is the centre of the British serpentine industry, where the locally-carved dark green stone veined with red, yellow and white streaks, is carved into an endless variety of ornaments, including lighthouses!

CHAPTER THIRTY THREE
ST ANTHONY'S HEAD

The 62ft tall octagonal tower.
TRINITY HOUSE

LONG BEFORE ST ANTHONY'S lighthouse was built by Trinity House in 1835, there had been a desperate need for a serious navigational aid at the eastern entrance to Falmouth harbour, also to keep ships clear of the Manacles.

Falmouth has the third deepest natural harbour in the world, and the deepest in western Europe.

In the seventeenth century, the Killigrew family displayed a large red flag from an elm tree denoting wind direction, but it was ordered to be taken down in 1779 because it was seen as a potential aid to invading ships.

The Manacles lie in the southern approach to Falmouth Harbour, near to Porthoustock.

St Anthony's lighthouse at the entrance to Falmouth Harbour.
TRINITY HOUSE

The wreck of the SS Mohegan.

Their name derives from 'church rocks' because the top of St Keverne church can be seen from their locality – somewhat ironic, because many sailors and ship passengers who lost their lives in wrecks on these rocks are buried there.

In a snowstorm on 22 January 1809, the two-year-old Royal Navy Cruiser class brig-sloop HMS *Primrose* came to grief on Mistrel Rock, with only one out of 126 people on board, the drummer boy, living to tell the tale. The same night, the transport ship *Dispatch*, returning home from Corunna with a detachment of the 7th Hussars on board, was also wrecked on the

A view of Carrick Roads from the lighthouse in the 1930s.
GREAT WESTERN RAILWAY

rocks, with 104 soldiers drowned and only seven men surviving the wreck.

St Anthony's lighthouse, which is 62ft tall and stands 72ft above mean high water was built by Olver of Falmouth, the same firm that built the lighthouse at Trevose Head. Olver began in 1834, and the first light was shone on 20 April the following year.

It also serves to warn ships off Black Rock in the centre of the channel leading into Falmouth Harbour. A two-storey keepers' house is attached.

Of course, a lighthouse can go a long way to preventing shipwrecks but cannot stop them altogether. On 14 October 1898, the brand new *SS Mohegan* en route from Tilbury to New York sank after hitting the Manacles, with the loss of 106 lives.

Initially the light was supplied by eight Argand oil lamps, but was changed to pressure vapour. It was electrified in 1954, when the fog bell was taken down and donated to a local church, being replaced by a modern fog horn on a platform.

The lighthouse was automated in 1987. The 1,500-watt occurring light with its first order fixed Fresnel lens shines white and red every 15 seconds, with a red sector for the Manacles. The white sector has an intensity of 210,000 candela and a range of 22 nautical miles, while the red sector has an intensity of 42,000 candela and a range of 20 nautical miles, while the fog horn sounds for three seconds once every 30 seconds.

CHAPTER THIRTY FOUR
MEVAGISSEY

THE FISHING PORT AND popular tourist destination of Mevagissey has its own harbour lighthouse.

Built in 1896, the 29ft tall white hexagonal cast-iron tower at the end of the south breakwater can be seen 12 miles across St Austell Bay, and has a focal range of 30ft.

Operated by the harbour authority, its white light shines in a sequence of 1.5 seconds on, two seconds off, 1.5 seconds on, and five seconds off. The foghorn emits a blast every 30 seconds.

Mevagissey's harbour lighthouse.
EDWARD WEBB*

Close-up view of the lantern.
DAN TAYLOR*

An early postcard view of fishing boats setting sail from the harbour.
ROBIN JONES COLLECTION

Pilchard fishing and smuggling were long the main sources of income for the inhabitants. Mevagissey boasted to being the first town in the country with electric street lighting, with its power station that began generating in 1895 using what else but pilchard oil to fuel it.

The harbour occupies the site of a medieval quay. The new port was empowered by an Act of Parliament in 1774, which led to the construction of the inner harbour, and its East and West quays. The outer harbour came in 1888, and was rebuilt in 1897 following severe damage in a blizzard six years earlier.

There are still more than 60 registered fishing boats active in Mevagissey today.

CHAPTER THIRTY FIVE
GRIBBEN HEAD

NEVER A LIGHTHOUSE as such, and looking every bit like the world's biggest stick of seaside rock, the Gribben Head daymark is one of the most distinctive navigational aids in Britain.

Trinity House built the 84ft tall square beacon tower on Gribben or Gribbin Head in 1832, so that sailors would no longer confuse the promontory at the eastern edge of St Austell Bay with either Dodman Point to the west or St Anthony's Head, and pass safely into Fowey, Par or Charlestown Harbour.

Many wrecks had occurred from the confusion before the daymark with its distinctive red-and-white stripes was built.

The headland is owned and administered by the National Trust, which holds summer open days when visitors can climb to the top of the tower via the internal staircase.

The Admiralty took over the daymark during World War Two and used it as a lookout station.

Below the headland to the east lies the little cove of Polridmouth. This is the heart of Daphne du Maurier Country: the author lived at nearby Menabilly House and then Kilmarth, and her international bestselling novel *Rebecca* was set here.

Dodman Point or the Dodman – the name comes from 'deadman' as it has been notorious for shipwrecks – also has a daymark erected as a navigational aid. In 1896 a local parson had a large granite cross erected to serve as a landmark for shipping, but two ships were still wrecked the following year. The last major tragedy here involved the pleasure boat *Darlwin* which sank in 1966 with the loss of all passengers.

The daymark on top of Gribben Head.
DARREN SHILSON

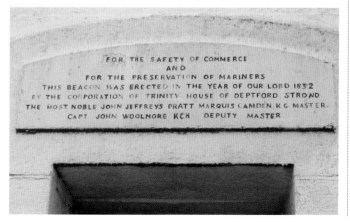

FOR THE SAFETY OF COMMERCE
AND
FOR THE PRESERVATION OF MARINERS
THIS BEACON WAS ERECTED IN THE YEAR OF OUR LORD 1832
BY THE CORPORATION OF TRINITY HOUSE OF DEPTFORD STROND
THE MOST NOBLE JOHN JEFFREYS PRATT MARQUIS CAMDEN K G MASTER
CAPT JOHN WOOLMORE KCH DEPUTY MASTER

The inscription above the daymark door. TONY ATKIN*

*A navigational aid, a barbershop
pole or a giant stick of rock?*
DARREN SHILSON

*The granite cross at Dodman Point on
the western edge of St Austell Bay.*
JOHN HORTON

CHAPTER THIRTY SIX
THREE SOUTH CORNWALL HARBOURS

BEYOND GRIBBEN HEAD LIES the entrance to Fowey Harbour, marked on the western edge by a 20ft tall round cast-iron lantern mounted on a short octagonal concrete base on the cliff edge at St Catherine's Point.

Dating from 1904, this navigational aid has a focal plane of 92ft. Its directional light shines for two seconds on, five seconds off, to the south east over the harbour entrance channel, with a red light to either side. The light is visible for 15 miles.

Further into the harbour, again on the west side, is Whitehouse Point, marked by a somewhat unusual cast iron 'drum' tower, comprising a cylindrical enclosure mounted on the top of a post and an external ladder to the enclosure, all painted bright red.

The light at St Catherine's Point.
CAPT MIKE SUTHERLAND/FOWEY
HARBOUR COMMISSIONERS

The approach to Whitehouse Pier with the red-painted light in the distance.
CAPT MIKE SUTHERLAND/FOWEY
HARBOUR COMMISSIONERS

Right: *The light at Whitehouse Pier.*
CAPT MIKE SUTHERLAND/FOWEY
HARBOUR COMMISSIONERS

Far right: *The tiny lighthouse at*
Spy House Point, Polperro.
NEIL DENHAM

The tiny St Catherine's beacon
overlooking the entrance to Fowey
harbour. CAPT MIKE SUTHERLAND/
FOWEY HARBOUR COMMISSIONERS

With a focal plane of 36ft, this directional light, which dates from 1894 but was acquired 'secondhand' and fixed at its present location at the end of Whitehouse Pier in 1904, flashes 1.5 seconds on, 1.5 seconds off. The light is white over the channel, red to the left and green to the right and can be seen for eight miles.

The Fowey Harbour Commissioners, which operate both lights, were established by an Act of Parliament in 1869 to develop and improve the town harbour, which received an enormous boost when a branch line linking it to the Cornwall Railway at Lostwithiel was opened, serving new deepwater jetties at Carne Point. It was followed in 1873 by the Cornwall Minerals Railway from Newquay and Par to more jetties between Caffa Mill Pill and Carne Point, making the town a major port for mineral exports, particularly china clay.

Apart from the clay ships, pleasure boating is big business in Fowey Harbour today.

Another tourist honeypot six miles to the east is the picture-postcard working fishing harbour of Polperro, crammed with painted fishermen's cottages, and long renowned for its shops selling pixies and their queen, Joan the Wad.

The harbour itself does not have a conventional lighthouse, although on the Western Pier there is a light on a stone structure which can be seen for four miles, a fixed white light which changes to red if the harbour is closed in bad weather. However, a tiny lighthouse is to be found a short walk along the coast path at Spy House Point to the east. Dating from 1911, and looking every bit like a miniature lighthouse, the 10ft round brick tower with an ordinary navigation light for its lantern has a focal plane of 98ft, and shows a right white or red light, depending on direction, and flashing three seconds on and three seconds off. The access door in the base, which makes it look like some form of Dr Who's Tardis-like structure, is no longer used now that the light is automated.

The harbour of Looe is a place you might well expect to find a conventional lighthouse, but you may well find yourself underwhelmed. The entrance to the harbour, at the end of Banjo Pier, which is shaped like its namesake musical instrument, carries just a bog-standard secondary light on a red 20ft tall iron column, with steps leading to a small metal balcony, and dating from the 1860s. The white occulting light is nonetheless sufficiently effective to be visible for 15 miles.

A fog signal house in a small white concrete building at Nailzee Point on the eastern side of the harbour emits two three-second blasts every 30 seconds.

To the west lies St George's or Looe Island, now run by the Cornwall Wildlife Trust and which can be visited by boat. Benedictine monks moved to the island and built a chapel there in 1139: they may have operated a basic beacon as a navigational aid.

Looe Island, made famous by its late owners, sisters Evelyn and Babs Atkins, who acquired it in 1965 and wrote the book We Bought an Island. *Monks may have established a rudimentary beacon there.* ROBIN JONES

Looe's Banjo Pier with the basic light post guiding ships in ROBIN JONES

CHAPTER THIRTY SEVEN
EDDYSTONE

Eddystone – the most famous of all British lighthouses and also the tallest, with its rooftop helipad.
TRINITY HOUSE

EDDYSTONE LIGHTHOUSE needs little introduction, for in its four or five incarnations, it has long been the most famous in Britain and probably the world too.

It stands on one of a group of rocks nine miles south west of Rame Head: nearer Cornwall than Devon, it nonetheless comes within Plymouth's city limits.

The red garnetiferous gneissic rocks had long been a major danger to shipping before businessman and inventor Henry Winstanley decided to build a lighthouse on them, after one of his five ships was wrecked there.

The proprietor of Winstanley's Waterworks, a major tourist attraction near Hyde Park, began work on building a wooden lighthouse at Eddystone's House Reef in 1696. His tower was anchored to the rock by 12 enormous iron stanchions.

The Admiralty provided him with a warship for protection as he carried out his labours. However, one day in June 1697, it failed to arrive, and a French privateer captured the inventor and took him as a prisoner to France.

Far from being grateful, Louis XIV was appalled, and ordered Winstanley's immediate release. Recognising the international importance of the lighthouse, the king said: "France was at war with England not with humanity".

The first light was shone from the 44ft tower on 14 November 1698. It was the world's first lighthouse to be built on an exposed rock in the open ocean.

Winstanley's lighthouse suffered extensive damage during its first winter, and so the entire top was rebuilt, making some historians consider the result to be a second lighthouse. What emerged in 1698 was a 12-sided tower with a stone-clad exterior on a timber framed construction with an octagonal top section.

Irked by critics who said the somewhat eccentric wooden design was too flimsy and decorative, Winstanley boasted that he was confident of spending a night on his lighthouse during a storm.

He visited the lighthouse on 27 November 1703 to complete modifications.

What nobody foresaw, however, was that his lighthouse was set to experience the worst storm ever recorded in southern England.

On 24 November, 120mph hurricane-force winds picked up and lasted until 2 December, causing widespread carnage. The great storm washed away Winstanley's improved Eddystone lighthouse, taking its designer with it, and thereby giving him a unique place in British lighthouse history.

Robinson Crusoe author Daniel Defoe wrote his first book, *The Storm*, detailing the "tempest that destroyed woods and forests all over England". Up to 15,000 people

Rule Britannia – with Eddystone lighthouse by her side. The reverse of the old British penny last issued in 1967. ROBIN JONES COLLECTION

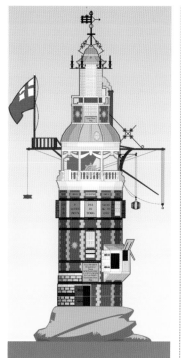

A modern depiction of Winstanley's ill-fated first lighthouse. HAWKEN KING*

Right: *Winstanley's improved version of his lighthouse, from a contemporary sketch.*

Far right: *Eddystone lighthouse in 1903, with the stump of Smeaton's tower alongside.* ROBIN JONES COLLECTION

John Smeaton, whose third lighthouse was stronger than the rock on which it stood.

were thought to have been killed. People thought it was an act of vengeance by God and the government accordingly declared 19 January 1704 to be a day of fasting.

Winstanley had nonetheless proven the great benefits of having a lighthouse on the deadly rocks.

He was followed by Captain John Lovett who acquired the lease of the rock for 99 years, also with the aim of charging fees from shipping.

Lovett selected John Rudyerd as his designer – a surprising choice, for he was a silk merchant and a property developer, not a scientist, engineer or architect. Born in Leek, Staffordshire, in 1650, he was the son of a wealthy landowner who had an established silk-trading business.

Rudyerd was given sole responsibility for the building of the new lighthouse in return for £250 a year for life.

He approached the design from the angle of a shipbuilder rather than a housebuilder, and devised a cone-shaped wooden tower, the tapering narrow design offering the least resistance to the sea. It was built round a ship's mast in the middle to give flexibility, and was covered with planks of wood coated with pitch to keep the water out.

A temporary light was lit from Rudyerd's 90ft tower in 1708 with the first permanent light following the next year.

Lovett died on 24 April 1710, leaving behind many unresolved financial problems regarding Eddystone. Rudyerd is thought to have died on 20 November 1718.

His lighthouse was hailed a major success, and it stood for 47 years. However, on the night of 2 December, 1755, the lantern top was set on fire, probably by a spark from one of the candles.

The 84 or 94-years-old keeper Henry Hall tried to fight the fire by throwing buckets of water upwards at it. The heat melted the lead roof of the lantern, and some of the molten metal spilled down his throat.

Hall and the other keeper were forced to retreat out on to the rock.

Isaac Sailmaker's contemporary illustration of Rudyerd's Eddystone lighthouse.

A Mr Edwards saw the calamity from the shore and organised a boat to rescue the keepers, arriving eight hours later. The sea was too rough – the name Eddystone refers to the currents and whirls that appear in the waters at this point – and so ropes were thrown to the keepers who were then dragged through the waves to safety. The fire lasted for five days and completely destroyed the lighthouse.

Hall died 12 days after the fire. A post mortem by a Dr Spry of Plymouth discovered a flat oval piece of lead weighing more than seven ounces in his stomach.

Spry's account of this discovery was disbelieved by the Royal Society. Defending his reputation, Spry set out on a campaign to prove them wrong, carrying out a series of bizarre experiments in which he poured molten lead down the throats of dogs and birds to show they could survive. The piece from Hall's stomach is displayed in the Royal Scottish Museum in Edinburgh.

Ship owners were desperate to replace the light, and Trinity House marked the rocks with a lightship in the meantime.

The next designer was Yorkshireman John Smeaton, who had been recommended for the job by the Royal Society.

His design was based on that of an oak tree, but built of stone, not wood. He needed the Royal Navy to desist from press-ganging his army of labourers in Plymouth, and so Trinity House agreed with the Admiralty to provide each of them with a special medal to show that they were engaged on the lighthouse.

Looking every bit like a Dalek, Winstanley's original Eddystone lighthouse featured on the 63p stamp in a Royal Mail series of lighthouse stamps in 1998. ROBIN JONES COLLECTION

Work began in 1756. To tackle the wet conditions on the Eddystone, Smeaton devised a quick-drying concrete, hydraulic lime which developed into what we now know as Portland cement.

Granite was used for the foundations and facing, with each block fastened to the next by dovetail joints and marble dowels. Smeaton also invented a crane-like device for hauling the huge blocks of stone from ships to considerable heights.

The end result was the world's first stone lighthouse tower out at sea. The first light, provided by 24 candles, was shone on 16 October 1759.

It was so tough that it could stand anything that the Channel weather threw at it. However, it proved to be far more resolute than the rock on which it was built, although the wooden part was badly damaged by fire in 1770 and was rebuilt four years later.

When cracks appeared in the rock supporting Smeaton's tower in the 1870s – every time a large wave hit the lighthouse, it shook from side to side - it was clear that a new lighthouse would have to be built, but on a neighbouring rock.

Nevertheless, as a monument to its builder's achievement, the top two thirds of the tower were taken down block by block and re-erected in 1882 on Plymouth Hoe, replacing a triangular obelisk erected as a navigational aid by Trinity House in the early nineteenth century.

The relocated tower was opened to the public by the Mayor of Plymouth on 24 September 1884 and has long been the city's most distinctive sea-front landmark and a tourist attraction. The Grade 1 listed tower is open for visitors who are allowed to climb the 93 steps to the lantern room and enjoy unrivalled views of Plymouth Sound and the city behind.

Photographer Dave Mitchell decided to fly a kite on Plymouth Hoe – with his camera fixed to it, and grabbed this seagull's eye view of Smeaton's Tower.
DAVE MITCHELL

Smeaton's Tower on the Hoe can be climbed by visitors. MAX HUGHES*

The remaining stump still stands on its rock alongside the current lighthouse as the foundations proved too strong to be dismantled.

Smeaton is today known as 'the father of civil engineering". It was Smeaton who thought up the term 'civil engineers' to distinguish them from military engineers graduating from the Royal Military Academy at Woolwich.

In 1771, he founded the Society of Civil Engineers, which was renamed the Smeatonian Society after his death, and evolved into today's Institution of Civil Engineers.

The current lighthouse was designed by Trinity House engineer-in-chief James Douglass. He drew on the development of Smeaton's techniques used by Robert Stevenson in Bell Rock lighthouse, which was built between 1807-10 12 miles off the coast of Angus, and is so solid that its masonry has not been improved on in two centuries.

In 1877, Douglass announced that Eddystone lighthouse would be rebuilt on a more solid foundation to the south east.

Douglass used bigger stone blocks than Smeaton and laid them in a way that they were not just dovetailed on all sides, but each course was dovetailed to the next.

The first light was shone from Douglass's 161ft tall tower through Fresnel lenses in 1882.

The original oil powered lamps were replaced in 1956 by electric versions.

The practice of lighthouse keepers catching fish by flying a kite from the balcony of their galleries was thought to originate from Eddystone. The kites held the line far enough away from the tower and rocks so that the line dropped straight into the water.

A helipad was installed in 1980 for future access by maintenance crews, for two years later, Eddystone became the first Trinity House rock station to be automated, the last keeper being Warren Seagrave. Controlled from Harwich, the light was switched back on following modernisation on 18 May 1982, 100 years to the day since the opening of Douglass's lighthouse by the then Duke of Edinburgh, who had laid the final stone.

The white light, powered by a 70-watt lamp with an intensity of 199,000 candela, flashes twice every 10 seconds and can be seen from 22 nautical miles away. It has a focal range of 134ft. A subsidiary fixed red light covers a 17 degree arc marking a treacherous reef called the Hands Deep. The fog signal sounds three blasts every 60 seconds.

Eddystone lighthouse is mentioned in Herman Melville's classic novel *Moby Dick*: "See what a real corner of the world it occupies; how it stands there, away off shore, lonelier than the Eddystone Lighthouse".

The lighthouse featured in the design of the old British pre-decimal penny, shining on the horizon behind the seated figure of Britannia.

In 1970, the lighthouse came to prominence again, when a band called Edison Lighthouse was hurriedly assembled to perform a song recorded by studio musicians under that banner. The song *Love Grows (Where my Rosemary Goes)* stayed at number one in the UK charts for five weeks and reached number five in the US Billboard charts.

CHAPTER THIRTY EIGHT
IN AND AROUND PLYMOUTH SOUND

RAME HEAD IS THE southern tip of the Rame peninsula, often referred to as Cornwall's 'forgotten corner" because most incoming visitors to the county pass it by without a second glance as they head for resorts further west. The peninsula is bordered by water on three sides in the form of the rivers Lynher and Tamar and Plymouth Sound.

The headland's strategic importance was recognised from earliest times, as evidenced by the remains of a sizeable Iron Age fort.

It was always a prominent landmark for both the seafarers and local fishermen leaving Plymouth, for it was both the last and first part of Devon they saw on their voyages. As such, it appears in the sea shanty *Spanish Ladies*, thought to date from the alliance between Britain and Spain against revolutionary France.

A slate chapel with a barrel-vaulted stone roof was built on the headland, possibly in the tenth century, and dedicated to St Michael the Archangel, as all buildings on similar high points have been. It may have been a much earlier Celtic hermitage, but no record, however of the chapel exists before 1397, and in 1425, it was granted a licence to hold mass every Monday and at Michaelmas.

Also in the fifteenth century, the Borough of Plymouth paid a watchman to maintain a beacon on the headland, and to give news of incoming vessels. It is likely that the little chapel was used in conjunction with this.

It is also recorded that in 1588, a pair of watchmen were paid to watch out for the Spanish Armada from Rame Head.

The little building was restored in 1882 for William Henry, 4th Earl of Mount Edgcumbe, but long ago reverted to a ruin.

At the entrance to Plymouth Sound lies a colossal feat of nineteenth-century nature-denying engineering, in the form of Plymouth breakwater, a structure that made the great naval port the city it is today.

In 1609, the Admiralty made Plymouth its base in south-west England, and shipping increased dramatically. So did wrecks, with numerous vessels driven by southerly gales across the Sound to smash to pieces on the shore at Bovisand.

On one day in 1804, ten ships were wrecked in the appropriately-named Deadman's Bay and even the shameless townsfolk who traditionally welcomed the rewards from such

The ruin of St Michael's chapel on Rame Head may have been a fifteenth-century 'lighthouse'. NICK HOMER

The lighthouse at the western end of Plymouth breakwater. NICK SAREBI*

The breakwater and Shovel Fort, with Bovisand and Heybrook Bay in the distance. MICK LOBB*

The beacon at the eastern end of the breakwater with its unique six-man basket. ROB FARROW*

wreckage began to demand that action was taken to stop the carnage.

The Admiralty suffered great embarrassment at the number of ships that came to grief only a few miles from its port. In 1806, it commissioned a study into the building of a breakwater that would turn the Sound into 1,000 acres of safe anchorage.

John Rennie and Joseph Whidbey were appointed engineers. Farmer's son Rennie was a Scottish civil engineer famous for designing many bridges, canals, and docks, while Whidbey achieved recognition in his own right as a naval engineer.

Helped by the master-attendant of the Plymouth Dockyard, a Mr Hemans, the pair designed a breakwater stretching between Bovisand and Cawsand bays along the line of the Panther, Shovell and St Carlos rocks, which extended to about 60ft deep.

The plan received approval by the Prince Regent on 22 June 1811, after which Admiralty ordered detailed plans to be drawn up.

The breakwater has a central portion of 1,000 yards and two arms each 350ft long and formed at an angle of 120 degrees to the main section, bending backwards to afford better protection of the anchorage that would be enclosed.

The design incorporated a solid wall that ended 10ft above the low water mark, and a 30ft wide top. It was built from rough-hewn blocks weighing between one half and two tons, along with some bigger ten-ton blocks, and the gaps between were filled with rubble.

To supply the 3.5 million tons of stone needed, a limestone quarry eventually covering 25 acres was opened at Oreston. The first limestone block weighed seven tons. It was taken to the site on one of ten specially-adapted sailing barges and dropped 30ft onto the seabed on Shovel Rock on August 8, 1812, the birthday of the Prince Regent.

Referred to as 'the great national undertaking', the project was seen as mammoth an undertaking in its day as the Channel Tunnel in the late twentieth century.

By the end of 1812, parts of the breakwater rose above the water, and three years later, it was decided to raise its top by another 10ft.

A bad storm in 1817 washed large amounts of rock away. Try as they might against successive storms, the builders could not achieve the 1-in-3 gradient of the breakwater design, eventually letting the sea dictate that it should be 1-in-5.

A railway was laid on the top of the breakwater for the movement of horse-drawn wagons carrying the stone.

A commemorative stone recalls the visit of Queen Victoria, as Princess Victoria, to the breakwater in August 1833.

The top part was paved over with granite and the project was finally complete in 1841, having taken three decades.

As the breakwater rose above the waves, it became as much of a hazard to shipping as the rocks had previously been, so it was clear that a lighthouse was needed. After complaints by city traders, one was erected at the western end of the breakwater, serving the busier of the two channels.

It was designed by Walker & Burgess and built out of white granite from Luxulyan in Cornwall. The building of the 78ft stone tower began on 22 February 1841 and was completed on 9 November 1843. The 8ft tall lantern had 118 mirrors, and with a focal plane of 63ft, the light is visible for 8 miles except during fog. The fog warning bell first installed in the lighthouse had been made for Notre Dame Cathedral in Montreal, Canada, but was found to be out of tune.

The first light was shone in June 1844. To mark the opening of the lighthouse, a packed horse-drawn omnibus was driven from end to end, accompanied by a military band.

Today, the light flashes every ten seconds, white flashes to the north-east for ships leaving the harbour and red flashes otherwise.

A second white light, flashing two seconds on, two seconds off, is shown over the entrance channel to the south west, from a lower window in the white-painted lighthouse, with a focal plane of 39ft. The fog horn sounds one blast every 15 seconds.

To save money, plans to build a similar lighthouse at the other end of the breakwater were scrapped, and it ended up with only a beacon, albeit a very unusual one. Built between June

The Ocean Court light overseeing the Hamoaze. ALEX TRABAS/ListofLights.org

The Queen Anne's Battery range rear light in Cattedown. ALEX TRABAS/ListofLights.org

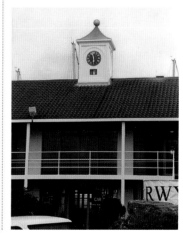

Striped marker beacon at Bovisand opposite the breakwater.
RON ALLDAY*

and November 1845, it comprises a wrought iron globe 6ft in diameter mounted on a wooden pole and 20ft above the high water mark. It was designed so that shipwrecked seamen might climb up the pole and get into the globe to wait until help arrived. The globe could contain six men, but it is not known if it has even been used as intended.

A concrete wave breaker was placed in position on the breakwater in 1871, to increase protection from stormy seas. A second one followed in 1928, after which many more wave breakers have been added.

During late Victorian times and in the early twentieth century, the breakwater was a favourite place for local families to have picnics! This has long since been disallowed.

The Shovel fort, which stands on the Shovel Rocks, is not physically linked to the breakwater despite its appearance from Plymouth Hoe, but stands 100ft away from its edge.

The illuminated breakwater was and still is a hazard to shipping. The barquentine *Yvonne* collided with the breakwater in September 1920 and became a complete loss, and a Lancaster bomber crashed into it following a raid on the submarine bases at L'Orient in 1944.

One of the world's first free-standing breakwaters, the mile-long breakwater may also be viewed as a giant manmade reef, although rocks have to be regularly dumped along it to counteract wave erosion. It is not a guaranteed permanent fixture.

Two more modern lights in Plymouth are worthy of note.

The first is the Queen Anne's Battery range rear light, which is shown from a small window in a square cylindrical clock tower on top of a two-storey building in Artillery Place off Teats Hill Road in Cattedown.

With a focal plane of 46ft, and like the breakwater lighthouse operated by Cattewater Harbour Commissioners, the occulting light flashes once every 7.5 seconds, showing white to the south-west over the channel, red to the left and green to the right.

Secondly, overlooking the modern Mayflower Marine in the Hamoaze, the name given to the section of the Tamar estuary passing Devonport, is a 10ft wooden tower on a platform on top of the Ocean Court condominium building in Richmond Walk. Its purpose is to guide approaching craft from the west.

It has a focal plane of 49ft, with quick-flashing lights, white, red or green depending on direction. The pyramidical tower is painted white with a red triangle acting as a daymark.

CHAPTER THIRTY NINE
START POINT

THE SOUTH HAMS OF DEVON are renowned for rolling hills, patchwork quilt fields, quaint thatched villages with wonderfully-atmospheric inns, narrow green lanes leading down to smuggler's coves and tidal creeks.

A sharp contrast to this idyllic pastoral image are the cliffs of the south coast, especially the jagged greenschist and mica-schist rocks that comprise the rugged landscape of Start Point, one of the most exposed peninsulas in England. Whereas the South Hams ooze homeliness, the Start can be hell.

The name means 'tail' and is apt because the headland juts out almost a mile into the sea. It is also to be found elsewhere, such as Stert Point opposite Burnham-on-Sea, and on an island off Sanday in the Orkney Islands, where there is another Start Point lighthouse, dating from 1806.

To ships, South Devon's Start Point is every bit as deadly as it looks. Even after a lighthouse was built on the headland in 1836, there have been frequent shipwrecks.

Start Point lighthouse, built on one of the most exposed headlands in England. TRINITY HOUSE

The circular tower, built of tarred and white-painted granite ashlar with a cast-iron lantern roofed in copper, itself has a decidedly Gothic touch. It was designed by James Walker to the architectural trend of his day, with its crenelated parapet. Walker built another 28 lighthouses, including, as we have seen, the first but unsuccessful Bishop Rock light.

Start Point's optic was a first for Trinity House. It was a type of dioptric apparatus designed by Alan Stevenson, best known for the optic at the Skerryvore lighthouse, which lies 12 miles off the coast of Tiree in western Scotland and at 156ft is the tallest in Britain.

The machinery was located in a small

On the edge of a precipice: Start Point lighthouse has stood here since 1836, but lost its fog signal station to subsidence in 1989. TRINITY HOUSE

Approaching Start Point from the coastal footpath from Great Mattiscombe Sand. ROD WARD

Approaching Start Point from the coastal footpath from Great Mattiscombe Sand. ROD WARD

The Start Point lighthouse lens. ROD WARD

building on the cliff face and relied on a weight falling in a tube running down the sheer cliff to operate it.

At first, a pair of white lights were shown, one revolving and the other fixed to mark the Skerries Bank. A fixed red subsidiary light still marks this danger.

In 1860, the light was supplemented by a fog bell, replaced by a siren in 1875.

A rough-hewn staircase in the cliffs led down to a small landing cove used by the keepers to go fishing in calm weather.

In 1871, the two middle floors of the 92ft tall tower were taken out and outside accommodation provided for the keepers inside the walled enclosure surrounding the tower.

One of the worst shipwrecks was that of the steamship *Marana*, in the Great Blizzard of 1891. The crew abandoned ship at Lannacombe Bay, but the lifeboat carrying 22 seamen was smashed to pieces near Prawle Point and only four crew members in a smaller lifeboat survived.

The lighthouse was electrified in 1959 and automated in 1993.

Subsidence led to the collapse of the fog signal house in December 1989, and its replacement by a free-standing stack.

The light, which stands 203ft above mean high water, has an intensity of 200,000 candela and a range of 25 nautical miles. The light comprises a white group flashing three times every ten seconds while the fog signal sounds once every 60 seconds.

While the withdrawal of keepers from most Trinity House lighthouses in this book has ended guided tours that they once offered to the public, an excellent visitor centre open during summer months has been established at Start Point.

Three of the four keepers' cottages are available as holiday lets.

CHAPTER FORTY
THE DART ESTUARY

THE ESTUARY OF THE River Dart has since time immemorial been a natural harbour of immense strategic naval importance because of its deep-water mooring.

Ships taking part in the Crusades to the Holy Land in 1147 and 1190 set sail from Dartmouth, and it has been a base of the Royal Navy since the time of Edward III, who granted a charter giving the port borough status.

Dartmouth's darker side was that it was also a base for privateering, a polite term for legalised piracy. One of its mayors, John Hawley, was a licensed privateer and is said to be the basis for Geoffrey Chaucer's Shipman in *The Canterbury Tales*.

The town figures prominently in England's regular feuds with its ancient enemy France:

The modern light at Kingswear.
ALEX TRABAS/ListofLights.org

The tower of the short-lived lighthouse at Dartmouth Castle, with Kingswear Castle on the opposite bank.
ROBIN JONES

*The 80ft granite daymark at
Frowards Point in winter.*
MARK LAKEMAN

Dartmouth was sacked twice during the Hundred Years' War.

It was Hawley who in 1388 built a small coastal fort at Dartmouth, which evolved into the present Dartmouth Castle, one of a pair guarding the river entrance, the other being the smaller Kingswear Castle on the opposite bank. A great chain was laid between the two every night to prevent incursions by hostile ships.

In 1856 the 50ft tall white-painted square tower now used for the castle shop and ticket office was built as a navigational aid to guide shipping into Dartmouth's harbour.

It showed a red fixed light from a height of 80ft visible 10 miles away. However, the light was not very useful, since the navigable channel is on the other side of the river entrance, and it became disused by at least 1886, and possibly two decades before. The building is now the Lighthouse Tearoom.

Kingswear too had a lighthouse, a 36ft octagonal stone tower, built into the side of the cliff in 1864, with a focal plane of 85ft, with a marker buoy off Lighthouse Beach in front of it.

This lighthouse was demolished in 1980 after it was declared unsafe, and replaced the following year by a modern squat round cylindrical tower 13ft high, mounted on top of a rock on the shore near the base of the old lighthouse, with a conical hooded lantern on the top. The light is shown through a window in the lantern.

Operated by the Dart Harbour and Navigation Authority, it has a focal plane of 30ft and its directional light flashes 1.5 seconds on, 1.5 seconds off. Its white light is shown in a south-westerly direction over the channel, green to the right and red to the left. It is said to be visible for nine nautical miles.

To the east at Frowards Point, stands an 80ft tall octagonal daymark 500ft above sea level, built of grey granite in 1864 by the Dart Harbour Commissioners.

*An incoming customs patrol passes
the modern Kingswear light, seen
on the shore just above the mast.*
ROBIN JONES

CHAPTER FORTY ONE
BERRY HEAD

UP TO NOW, WE HAVE seen some of the tallest lighthouses in Britain. Now we come to the shortest.

At just 16ft tall, Berry Head lighthouse near Brixham is as a building lower than any other Trinity House lighthouse in the country, because it does not need to be any higher than the great limestone headland on which it stands.

Yet at 190ft above sea level, it also claims to be the highest.

Furthermore, it is said to be the deepest, because the lantern optic was originally turned by the action of a weight falling down a 148ft deep shaft, a method made redundant by a small motor.

Semaphore signalling apparatus had been installed on Berry Head before 1875 and acted as the Lloyd's signal station for Torbay.

The lighthouse, which stands beyond Berry Head coastguard station and oversees the

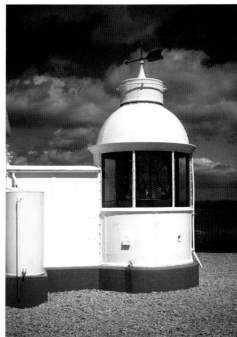

Berry Head's tiny lighthouse. TORBAY COAST & COUNTRYSIDE TRUST

An early twentieth-century view of the lighthouse and its staff. TRINITY HOUSE

The complex of lighthouse buildings on the headland. TORBAY COAST & COUNTRYSIDE TRUST

approaches to the safe sheltered harbours of Torbay and Brixham Roads, was built in 1906, near to defences built in 1793 on the site of an iron age hill fort to protect the ports against potential invasion from revolutionary France.

The light was converted to automatic acetylene operation in 1921 and adapted to mains electricity in 1994.

Its white group flashes twice every 15 seconds, and it has an intensity of 9,000 candela with a range of 14 nautical miles.

The headland also has an omnidirectional radio range/distance measuring equipment beacon for air traffic control.

Berry Head, bought by Torbay Borough Council in 1969 and designated as a country park a year later, is also a National Nature Reserve because of its many rare and threatened species which depend on the limestone soils, mild climate and exposed conditions of the headland.

The view out to sea from the top of Berry Head. TORBAY COAST & COUNTRYSIDE TRUST

CHAPTER FORTY TWO
BRIXHAM HARBOUR

BRIXHAM HAS ONE OF the largest fishing fleets in Britain, with more than 100 vessels, both large beam trawlers and smaller day boats, landing their catch and selling it at the market on the quayside.

Known as the 'Mother of Deep-Sea Fisheries', its boats helped the development of fishing at the major centres of Lowestoft, Hull and Grimsby, and many developments in the design of fishing trawlers were made here.

The song *Red Sails In The Sunset* was inspired by Brixham trawlers. The sails were red because they were dyed with ochre, a mineral found in Brixham and, after boiling with oak bark, tar and tallow, protected the canvas from salt water. A paint made from ochre was invented in Brixham in the 1840s and was the world's first application to prevent rust on cast iron.

However, over the centuries, many ships came to grief on nearby rocks. During a storm on 10 January 1866, when the sailing boats could not return to harbour, and the beacon on the breakwater was swept away, the fishermen's wives lit a huge bonfire on the quay as a replacement navigational aid. Nonetheless, 50 ships were lost and more than 100 men drowned.

The disaster led to the first Brixham lifeboat being installed in 1866.

The outer harbour breakwater, popular with sea anglers, together with the headland of Berry Head, offer protection for the huge number of boats that use the harbour. The limestone quarried locally to build the breakwater as well as houses was also used at Dagenham to make steel for Ford cars.

A lighthouse was established on the breakwater around 1878, but the present lighthouse at the far end was built around 1916. It has a focal plane of 30ft.

Operated by Tor Bay Harbour Marine Services, the white 20ft cylindrical cast iron tower with lantern and gallery has an occulting light which shines for three seconds every 15 seconds. It can be accessed by walking along the breakwater.

The lighthouse at the end of Brixham's breakwater. HERBYTHYME*

Fishing trawlers safely berthed in Brixham Harbour. COLIN HOWLEY*

CHAPTER FORTY THREE
TEIGNMOUTH AND SHALDON

Teignmouth's sea front lighthouse was built in 1845. TONY VOLANTE

The rear range light on the front of Lynton House Hotel.
LORRAINE LUNN

THE 'TWIN' SETTLEMENTS of Teignmouth and Shaldon have three lights between them.

Teignmouth's classic lighthouse, a round limestone tower built in 1845 on the quay at Den Point has been described as a 'toy' lighthouse because of its compact size, just 20ft tall, with a focal plane of 33ft.

It forms the front light of a pair of range lights, the other being a small lantern fixed to the top of a 37ft street-lamp-style black post outside the Lynton House Hotel in Powderham Terrace.

Incoming ships must line up the Powderham Terrace light with the classic lighthouse in order to turn safely into the estuary of the River Teign.

The lighthouse shows a continuous red light and is visible for about six miles.

Both lights are operated by Teignmouth Harbour Commission.

The story of the lighthouse duo dates back to the emergence of Teignmouth as a serious port for the export of Dartmoor granite and ball clay from the mines north of Newton Abbot.

Teignmouth's first quay, known as the Old Quay, was built in the mid-eighteenth century, and the opening of James Templar's Stover Canal in 1792 gave it a massive boost. Barges brought huge quantities of ball clay down from the mines to the quay, from where it was shipped out for use in the potteries springing up around Stoke-on-Trent.

In 1820, the Haytor Granite Tramway, a horse-drawn railway where the track was carved from granite blocks and the wagons pulled by horses, was built by Templar's son George, linking the granite quarries at Haytor to the canal and in turn Teignmouth. Haytor granite brought down by wagon and barge to Teignmouth was used to build a new London Bridge, amongst many other illustrious buildings.

With mineral trade booming, and sizeable

Lighthouse and the Ness, Teignmouth. VALENTINE'S SERIES.

quantities of coal, timber and culm coming in, the Teignmouth Harbour Commission saw that the shifting sand and dangerous currents in the entrance to the quay where the Teign meets the English Channel would jeopardise the bigger loaded ships, even those with experienced pilots.

So in 1845 the lighthouse was built on the sea front, with the Earl of Devon paying the surveyor's fee. Despite early criticism that the light was not strong enough, the little lighthouse is still giving sterling service today.

Shaldon has a distinctive navigational aid which looks like a lighthouse in miniature, but is only a beacon. Nonetheless, it is a much-loved landmark and features on the village sign.

The Phillip Lucette beacon is a stone column standing 15ft high on the beach off Marine Parade, with a focal plane of 13ft, and its red occulting light which flashes once every six seconds has a range of three miles.

Its purpose is also to act as a guide for ships entering the estuary and is also operated by Teignmouth Harbour Commission.

Above left: An early twentieth-century postcard of Teignmouth lighthouse. ROBIN JONES COLLECTION

Above right: The Philip Lucette beacon which guides boats into the Teign estuary from the Shaldon side. PAUL DICKSON

The little Shaldon beacon with Teignmouth in the background. ROB BREWER

CHAPTER FORTY FOUR
PORTLAND BILL

Lighthouse visitor Thomas Hardy, the novelist who made the Dorset landscape his own.

The Lower lighthouse is now a bird observatory, with a 'new' lantern.
ROBIN JONES

THE ISLE OF PORTLAND, the great chunk of white stone jutting out into the English Channel at the end of the great ridge of pebbles known as Chesil Beach was likened to a 'Gibraltar of the North' by Dorset novelist Thomas Hardy, who referred to it in his works as the Isle of Slingers.

To the north of the isle lie the havens of Weymouth and Portland. However, over the centuries, countless sailors have perished trying to reach them.

The danger is presented by the Portland Ledge, an underwater Portland stone feature which projects into the sea from the Bill of Portland and forms the Shambles sandbank.

Disrupting the tidal flow, it creates a tidal race to the south of Portland Bill known as the Portland Race and which can reach speeds of 13ft per second at spring tides.

At Portland Bill, caves have been carved out of the rock by the sheer force of the Channel waves.

A decent navigational aid had been needed for centuries, and a beacon shone on the headland from around 1620, but it was not until 1669 that Sir John Clayton was empowered

The Isle of Portland's most-photographed landmark is Portland Bill lighthouse. ROBIN JONES

Above left: *The Lower lighthouse around the beginning of the twentieth century, with its original lantern.* ROBIN JONES COLLECTION

Above right: *Old Higher lighthouse owner Dr Marie Stopes at work in her laboratory in 1904.*

to build a lighthouse.

Nothing came of his scheme, and seafarers waited until the early eighteenth century when Captain William Holman, petitioned Trinity House for the provision of a lighthouse. Astonishingly, Trinity House opposed the move, backed by the townsfolk and traders of Weymouth, saying that there was no need for a light there.

Weymouth folk refused to give in and on 26 May 1716, Trinity House finally obtained a patent for a Portland lighthouse from George I.

The rights to the lighthouse were leased to a private consortium which in 1716 built a pair of range lighthouses with enclosed lanterns and coal fires.

However, the lights were poorly maintained, and sometimes did not shine at all. A site visit by sea from two members of the Trinity House board in 1752 found that neither lighthouse shone until two hours after sunset.

After the lease ended and Trinity House compulsorily purchased the lights, it contracted Weymouth builder William Johns to take down one of the lighthouses and build a new one, which would also serve as a daymark.

In August 1788, it became the first lighthouse in England to be equipped with Argand oil lamps. At first, the lighthouse had two rows of them, with seven lamps in each row, and fitted with highly-polished reflectors, it was the first in the world to have a true reflector.

The lighthouse was visited by King George III during one of his frequent trips to Weymouth. During 1798, a pair of 18 pound cannons were installed at the lighthouse in case Napoleon Bonaparte tried to invade.

In 1844, a 23ft tall white stone obelisk was installed at the southern tip of Portland Bill as a warning of a low stone shelf extending 98ft out to sea.

The lighthouse was rebuilt in 1869, when a new Low lighthouse was constructed.

In its new format, the Higher lighthouse comprised a 40ft white-painted circular stone tower with lantern and gallery, attached to a keeper's cottage, with a second keeper's house nearby.

It was deactivated in 1906, when Trinity House decided to build a new single tower for Portland Bill, and sold it off privately.

Dr Marie Stopes, the pioneer of birth control, owned the property, which became known as the Old Higher lighthouse, from 1923 until 1958. Her guests included none other than Hardy himself, the playwright George Bernard Shaw and science fiction writer H.G. Wells. She rented it to naval officers during World War Two, when one of the visitors was a young up-and-coming ballerina, Margot Fonteyn.

The lighthouse became derelict in the sixties and was bought in 1981 by the present owners, Fran and Les Lockyer. It has been restored in keeping with its character, and Branscombe Lodge Cottage, a restored old paraffin store is now available for hire as a holiday let. Guests can enjoy spectacular views from the lighthouse tower.

The Lower lighthouse, an 82ft white-painted round stone tower with lantern and gallery, an annexe and separate keeper's cottage, was also decommissioned in 1906. Later, the lantern was removed, and the keepers' houses were used as a tearoom for many years.

The lighthouse and its attendant buildings in Portland Bill Road were in 1961 converted into a migrating bird observatory and ecological field station.

Run as Portland Bird Observatory and Field Centre, it is possible to stay both in the lighthouse and keeper's cottages, although the tower is open only to guests and observatory members.

The present operational Portland Bill lighthouse, a 136ft round sandstone tower standing sentinel above the

Aerial view of the Old Higher lighthouse complex. FRAN LOCKYER

This obelisk near the present-day lighthouse acts as a daymark.
ROBIN JONES

headland about half a mile south of the 1869 lighthouses, is unmistakeable, a classic image of "what a lighthouse should look like."

Automated on 18 March 1996, it emits between one and four flashes within a 20-second period, depending on direction, from its rotating Fresnel lens, and has an intensity of 635,000 candela and a range of 25 nautical miles. The foghorn sounds one 3.5-second blast every 30 seconds.

Trinity House has opened a visitor centre in the lighthouse, and offers guided tours during the summer.

The 1844 obelisk is threatened by erosion, but plans by Trinity House to move it in 2002 were axed due to public opposition.

In 1983, ITV screened *The Adventures of Portland Bill*, an animated children's television series set in a fictional lighthouse called Guillemot on the south coast of England, which bore an uncanny likeness to the real Portland Bill lighthouse.

Portland Bill was a lighthouse keeper, Mrs Lundy owned a cottage on the mainland and Eddy Stone ran the village shop!

The Old Higher lighthouse today.
FRAN LOCKYER

CHAPTER FORTY FIVE
PORTLAND HARBOUR AND WEYMOUTH

PORTLAND HARBOUR IS ONE of the deepest manmade harbours in the world at between 39ft and 66ft deep, and one of the largest, with a surface of 2,125 acres.

The first harbour here came into existence because the Dorset coast at Weymouth, backed by the great shingle ridge of Chesil Beach and the lofty mass of the Isle of Portland, gave natural protection to ships in the worst of weathers, apart from storms coming in from the south east. It was of such strategic importance that Henry VIII built Portland Castle and Sandsfoot Castle to defend it.

The modern harbour dates from 1849 when the Royal Navy built the landmark breakwater using blocks of Portland stone. It took until 1872 to complete it, and at last it eliminated the harbour's Achilles' heel by giving protection from south-easterly winds.

At the same time, a string of fortifications including the Verne Citadel fort, Nothe Fort, High Angle Battery, East Wear Battery and two forts on the breakwaters were constructed.

Two further breakwaters were added in 1906 to reduce the threat from potential torpedo attacks from the east. In 1914, HMS *Hood* was deliberately sunk across the southern entrance

The 1905 skeletal cast-iron tower at Portland Harbour breakwater's 'A' head. NICK MUTTON

View of Chesil Beach, Portland Harbour's western side, well behind the breakwaters, from Fortuneswell at sunset. ROBIN JONES

The breakwater 'B' head light.
JIM LINWOOD*

Standing at the end of the breakwater's 'C' head is a 36ft tall concrete tower topped by a light mast.
JIM LINWOOD*

to the first breakwater, to form a barrier against enemy submarines, and still lies there today.

The navy sold off the harbour in 1996, after which it became a water sports centre and a service station for channel shipping. It is used by a huge variety of vessels, from cruise liners to tankers and container carriers.

The four-section breakwater has several lights, all controlled by the harbour authority. The one on the 'A' head, the detached north-east breakwater, comprises a 70ft high white-painted hexagonal skeletal cast-iron lighthouse. It replaced a stone lighthouse dating from 1851 and which was removed when this pier was extended.

Dating from 1905, it is the only operational survivor in England of a kind of once-common kind of prefabricated navigational aid, and can be reached only by boat, but the site is not open to the general public.

With a focal range of 71ft, the light which flashed white every ten seconds can be seen for 14 miles.

At the northern entrance to the harbour, on the breakwater's 'B' head, is a 26ft square concrete tower with a mast on top holding a red occulting light, which flashes once every 15 seconds, and which has a focal range of 36ft.

A similar arrangement exists on the 'C' head opposite, which has a green light occulting once every 10 seconds. There is also a light marking the south entrance.

CHAPTER FORTY SIX
ST ALBAN'S HEAD

The little chapel of St Aldhelm on St Alban's Head may well have been used as a beacon. JIM CHAMPION*

The former coastguard station now manned by volunteers. STEPHEN WILLIAMS*

THE TINY NORMAN CHAPEL which stands on St Alban's Head, a very much isolated section of the Jurassic Coast near Worth Matravers, has given rise to much conjecture over the years.

One school of thought is that it was more than a place of worship, maybe an out station of Corfe Castle to provide extra defensive capability: this reasoning is supported by the similarity of construction details between the pair.

Recent repairs to the roof have suggested, though not proven, that it may have been used centuries ago as a beacon. Where there may have once been fixed an iron basket to warn passing sailors, there is now a modern cross. Such use would tie in with other ecclesiastical buildings we have already seen elsewhere.

The little chapel is also believed to have been built on a much earlier Christian building, and it is widely conjectured that it has links with the seventh-century St Aldhelm, first Bishop of Sherborne, to which it is dedicated: a similar early Christian enclosure has been identified lying beneath Sherborne Old Castle. The name of the headland is a corruption of Aldhelm.

Nobody knows exactly why or when it was built. A local legend relates that in 1140 a bride and groom were sailing round the headland, when a sudden storm caused the boat to sink and both were drowned. The bride's father, who was watching from the cliffs, then built the chapel in their memory, and ordered a light to always be kept burning to warn other seamen.

The chapel was first mentioned in the thirteenth century. It may have been built as a chantry, where mass for the safety of sailors would be celebrated. Such chantries were suppressed during the reign of Edward VI, and by 1625, it was described as being used as a sea mark.

The chapel became a ruin, but the owners of Encombe House slowly repaired it during the nineteenth century, and on 18 July 1874, it was reopened as a place of worship.

Around this time, the chapel was the destination of an annual Whit Thursday procession from Worth Mattravers, where villagers would dress the building with flowers and dance inside, while making a secret wish.

In 1965, the chapel was given to Worth Matravers Parochial Church Council. The chapel was declared a Scheduled Monument in 2000.

CHAPTER FORTY SEVEN
ANVIL POINT, SWANAGE

OUR MARATHON JOURNEY around the lighthouse-heavy coast of the West Country ends at Anvil Point in Durlston County Park, a pleasant two-mile walk along the cliffs from Swanage.

Opened in 1881 by Joseph Chamberlain, Minister of Transport and father of Neville 'peace in our time' Chamberlain, the lighthouse, built of local Purbeck stone, was designed as a waypoint for vessels on passage along the English Channel coast.

Its light gives a clear line from Portland Bill to the west, and guides ships away from the three-mile reef off Hengistbury Head known as Christchurch Ledge and leads them into the Solent.

Looking out to sea from the lantern on Anvil Point. TRINITY HOUSE

Anvil Point lighthouse and keeper's cottages in Durlston Country Park. TRINITY HOUSE

Hand-coloured Edwardian view of Anvil Point.
ROBIN JONES COLLECTION

The westernmost measured nautical mile marker in Durlston Country Park. JIM CHAMPION*

The cylindrical tower with lantern and gallery, painted white with green trim and which stands in its complex at the end of Lighthouse Road stands at just over 39ft high, while the focal plane is 149ft.

The original Fresnel lens is on display in the Optics Gallery of the Science Museum in London. It now has a 250mm rotating optic.

The light was originally illuminated by a paraffin vapour burner, but in 1960 the station was modernised and converted from oil to mains electricity. It was automated on 31 May 1991.

Now equipped with a 1,000-watt filament lamp, and with an intensity of 500,000 candela, a white flash is shown every ten seconds. The light has a range of 24 nautical miles.

The old fog signal, a five-minute cannon, was replaced in 1981 by new automatic equipment, which bears a resemblance somewhat to Tater Du lighthouse with its array of panels. The fog signal has now been discontinued.

The keepers' houses are available as holiday lets.

Throughout this book, I have referred to the range of lighthouses, the distance from which they can be seen, in nautical miles. Here, in the last chapter, is a physical explanation, for in the country park, are two masts which mark a measured nautical mile, and which can be used by ships at sea to gauge their speed.

International agreement defines a nautical mile as a unit of length corresponding approximately to one minute of arc of latitude along any meridian, approximately 6,076 feet (1,852 metres), or 1.15 statute miles, the length of which is 5,280ft.

The nautical mile remains in use by sea and air navigators because of its convenience when working with charts constructed on the Mercator projection, the scale of which varies by around a factor of six from the equator to 80 degrees north or south latitude, making it therefore impossible to show a single linear scale for use on maps or charts smaller than about 1:80,000.

The international nautical mile derives from a "sea mile", which, in English usage, is the length of one minute of latitude at that latitude. It varies from approximately 6046.26ft at the Equator to around 6107.94ft at the poles, with an average length of 6077.1ft.

Similar sets of marker masts can be seen at Talland Bay and at Hannafore near Looe in Cornwall.

We began with an 'A' and have now ended with an 'A', but I am sure you will agree Anvil Point presents a very different perspective on life than that of Avonmouth, where we began our journey.